Tom Ambrose is a writer and historian. His recent books include *The Nature of Despotism: From Caligula to Mugabe, the Making of Tyrants* (2008), *Godfather of the Revolution* (2008) and *Prinny and his Pals* (2009), a re-evaluation of the character of George IV.

HEROES
AND EXILES
Gay Icons Through The Ages

Tom Ambrose

NEW
HOLLAND

Published in 2010 by New Holland Publishers (UK) Ltd
London • Cape Town • Sydney • Auckland
www.newhollandpublishers.com
Garfield House, 86–88 Edgware Road, London W2 2EA, United Kingdom
80 McKenzie Street, Cape Town 8001, South Africa
Unit 1, 66 Gibbes Street, Chatswood, NSW 2067, Australia
218 Lake Road, Northcote, Auckland, New Zealand

10 9 8 7 6 5 4 3 2 1

ISBN 978 1 84773 468 6

Publishing Director: Rosemary Wilkinson
Publisher: Aruna Vasudevan
Project Editor: Julia Shone
Editor: Fiona Plowman
Design and cover design: 2M Design
Production: Melanie Dowland
DTP: Tammy Warren

Reproduction by Pica Digital (Pte) Ltd, Singapore
Printed and bound in India by Replika Press

The paper used to produce this book is sourced from sustainable forests.

CONTENTS

INTRODUCTION:
THE FALL FROM GRACE

There can be few more harrowing accounts of institutional cruelty against blameless individuals than the persecution endured for centuries by male and female homosexuals in Western society. Once the most respected members of ancient Greek society, male homosexuals suffered an astonishing and irrational fall from grace with the coming of Christianity.

Heroes and Exiles is primarily concerned with both the fate and accomplishments of certain highly talented individuals, male and female, who found themselves in exile because of their homosexuality. Among them are the Italian Renaissance artist Benvenuto Cellini (1500–71), Queen Christina of Sweden (1626–89; queen of Sweden 1644–54), the English romantic poet Lord Byron (1788–1824), the Irish playwright Oscar Wilde (1854–1900) and the American novelist James Baldwin (1924–87). Some were driven into exile; others chose to flee to escape the condemnation and harassment of their societies. Whatever their personal reasons for exile, all these men and women showed great courage in refusing to allow either themselves or their creative achievements to be extinguished by bigots, many of whose very names are now forgotten.

The very idea of stigmatizing anyone because of his or her sexuality might seem ridiculous to many of us today and would have seemed strange to the people of ancient Greece around the year 500 BC. In a society where even the gods – Zeus, Dionysus and Aphrodite – indulged in love affairs with both sexes, mere mortals were similarly unconstrained by modern sexual convention. This was the golden age of male homosexuality, when same-sex love was accepted as normal and an older man could, with public approval, take a younger man as his pupil and lover, in what would later become known as 'Greek Love'. Strict laws governed such relationships. These laws were so strict, in fact, that in 399 BC, the philosopher Socrates (469–399 BC) was executed on a charge of corrupting the Athenian youth by inducing boys into prostitution – although this charge was, in fact, politically motivated due to Socrates's association with opponents of the democratic regime. Although often expressed in a physical manner, the purpose of the Greek Love relationship was primarily a spiritual and intellectual one, the older man acting as mentor and the younger as his pupil. To the John Addington (A. J.) Symonds (1840–93), writing centuries later and a man who had experienced firsthand the vindictiveness of homophobia in Victorian England, this was a lost ideal of loving responsibility by which:

> the lover taught, the hearer learned; and so from man to man was handed down the tradition of heroism ... love was maintained among the Spartans with a view to education ... the lover might represent his friend in the Assembly. He was answerable for his good conduct, and stood before him as a pattern of manliness, courage and prudence.

Greek Love also provided the emotional bonding for the most renowned military force in ancient Greece, the Theban Band, an elite regiment of 300 homosexual warriors sworn to defend each other to the death. Their leader Epaminondas (c.410–362 BC) was widely acknowledged as the greatest warrior and statesman of the age. According to the Greek historian Diodorus Siculus (1st century BC), he had two male lovers, Asopichus and Caphisodorus. So close were the three men, that when Epaminondas and Caphisodorus were killed in the Battle of Mantinea, in 362 BC, their comrades placed them in the same grave, a custom usually strictly reserved for husband and wife. At the Battle of Charonea in 338 BC against the Macedonians the Theban Band suffered its first and only defeat. The warriors fought with an astonishing bravery, comparable to that of the Spartans at the Battle of Thermopylae, in 480 BC standing their ground until every man lay dead. Their invincible courage so impressed the victor, Philip II of Macedon (382–336 BC; king of Macedon 359–336 BC), that he ordered a statue of a lion to be erected in their honour.

Yet, the most celebrated exponents of Greek Love were the heroes Aristogiton and Harmodius whose self-sacrificing courage in slaying the tyrant Hipparchus, in 514 BC, in defence of Athenian democracy against the actions of a tyrant was one of the most important symbolic acts in all Greek history. Harmodius and Aristogiton were hailed as martyrs to the cause of Athenian freedom. The famous sculptor, Antenor (c.540–500 BC), was given the first-ever commission paid for by public funds to create a bronze statue in their honour, known as 'The Tyrannicides'. This became the shrine of Athenian democracy, in the manner that the Statue of Liberty in New York would later become the symbol of American freedom. Other male lovers, such as Melanippus and Chariton, were similarly elevated to the heroic pantheon. The importance of these near canonizations cannot be over emphasized, for at no other time in history would homosexuality be so closely equated with heroism and civic responsibility. The acclaimed Roman philosopher Plato (428–348 BC) in the *Symposium*, was even prepared to argue that the very absence of male love in a society, such as that of the Persians, indicated just how truly barbaric, despotic and morally worthless they were.

Greek Love also existed between older and younger women, often beginning at *thiasoi* or academies, with young girls forming intimate friendships with the female tutors who taught them music, dancing and poetry. Just as homosexuality was thought to have inspired the young male warriors of Greece to acts of bravery in the defence of liberty, so was lesbianism seen to encourage creative genius among young women. The most famous of all lesbians, the poet Sappho (c.630–570 BC) was herself a teacher on the island of Lesbos. Sappho was married and like her male compatriots, found no incongruity in combining her social role as a wife with her same-sex liaisons. As the Greek biographer Plutarch (AD 46–119) wrote wisely of these times:

No sensible person can imagine that the sexes differ in matters of love as they do in matters of clothing. The intelligent lover of beauty will be attracted to beauty in whichever gender he [or she] finds it.

With the rise of Roman power, attitudes towards homosexuality changed and the master–pupil system of Greek Love fell into disfavour. Homosexuality still remained free of any social or legal control, however.

After establishing itself as a martial and highly efficient state, Rome gradually became more relaxed and libertarian in its views and behaviour. The English historian Edward Gibbon (1737–94), writing in the 18th century, claimed that of the first 12 Roman emperors only Claudius (10 BC–AD 54) was exclusively heterosexual and was even criticized by his own historian, Suetonius (AD 69–c.122), for being too narrow in his sexual tastes. Male marriage also became popular: the Emperor Nero (AD 37–68), in AD 65, married Sporus, a beautiful young man. Nor was this an isolated event, for the poet Juvenal (c.AD 55–127) laconically recorded a similar episode in his diary the following year on meeting a celebratory procession in the street: 'nothing special: just a friend marrying another man and a small group is attending'.

After Emperor Constantine (d.411) converted to Christianity in AD 313 the tolerance, and even disinterest, shown to homosexuality in the ancient world was swept away by the rise of Christianity. The Church's basis for attacking homosexuality appeared to be a single verse from the Book of Leviticus in the Old Testament that appeared to order the persecution of sodomites. In reality the newly triumphant Church sought to dominate and control every aspect of human life, including the sexual sphere.

As there were no divine rules that could be applied to homoeroticism, it had to be banned and those who disobeyed the Church command were persecuted. Soon sexual relations between males were forbidden as 'against nature' and death or banishment became the standard punishment for such a crime. The sons of Constantine continued this harsh treatment and in AD 341 a more comprehensive act forbidding sodomy was introduced, followed by the toughest legislation of all. New acts instituted by Theodosius the Great (AD 347–395) in AD 390 specifically prescribed death for those who had taken the passive role in sodomy. Fifty years later, execution by burning became the standard punishment for the same offence, followed, under the Emperor Justinian (485–565), by legislation making any form of homosexual activity a capital offence. Apparently these sanctions did not apply to emperors for a chronicler at the time of Emperor Constantine V (718–775) accuses him of having 'impious lust for men' and Michael III (836–867) was said to have fallen in love with one of his own courtiers, Basil the Macedonian.

Fervent Christians, once persecuted themselves, now became the persecutors and attacked the newly reviled minority, the sodomites. Rome's conversion to Christianity led to a reign of terror in which homosexuals were made the scapegoats for everything that went wrong in communities. From defeat in war, to crop failures and other natural disasters, homosexuals were wholly responsible for bringing down God's wrath on their innocent neighbours. In their role as universal scapegoats, gay people and Jews had much in common, both groups becoming targets for communal bullying. This campaign was enthusiastically endorsed by such eminent Christian leaders as St Augustine who declared that sodomy was a far greater sin for a man to commit than having carnal knowledge of his own mother and that as long as human nature was defiled by this appalling vice the Son of Man would never return to Earth.

As the historian William Percy (b.1933) wrote:

> Sodomy became ... the object of a thousand obscene fantasies. It was nowhere, yet everywhere threatened society with destruction. It was blotted out of the annals of the past, unrecorded in the present, forbidden to exist in the future. Trial records were burned along with culprits, so that no trace should remain. Yet enveloped in the impenetrable darkness of ignorance and superstition, it existed silent and unseen, a phantom eluding the clutches of an intolerant world.

Some of the myths that spread about homosexuals were extraordinary and credible only to an ignorant and deeply superstitious people. One chronicler, Peter the Chanter (d.1197) claimed that St Jerome had testified that as the Virgin Mary was giving birth to Jesus all the sodomites in the world suddenly died.

Throughout the Dark Ages the homophobic campaign continued, culminating in 1051, when St Peter Damian (1007–72) accused his own homosexual monks and priests of wanting to tear down the ramparts of the heavenly Jerusalem and replace them with the walls of accursed Sodom. The sentiment against homosexuals was given greater impetus by the very real threat of an Islamic invasion of Western Europe at the time and the widespread belief that Muslims were enthusiastic sodomites. Faced with such a threat, a conference was hastily convened in January 1120 at Nablus in the new Kingdom of Jerusalem at which King Baldwin II (1130–62) urged the delegates to ensure that all convicted sodomites – Catholic or Muslim, active or passive – should be burned alive. Even the victim of male rape suffered the same fate unless he could prove that he had cried out for help.

The justification for what seems an absurdity was the teachings of St Thomas Aquinas (1225–74) in his influential work *Summa Theologiae*, which became the standard repository of Catholic orthodoxy for almost a thousand years. Aquinas believed that 'the natural' should be the sole criterion used to judge sexual behaviour and that sins against nature were inspired by perverted lust. Animals, he argued, did not indulge in same-sex activity, unaware that later zoological research would prove him wrong. At the bottom of his ladder of evil was masturbation because it involved the sacrilegious spilling of seed. Above that was any deviation from the standard 'missionary position' in heterosexual intercourse – and at the very top were homosexuality and bestiality. Another of Aquinas's convictions was that sodomy was highly addictive and that every man was open to that temptation. Sodomites might be small in number, he argued, but they had the potential to contaminate the whole of male society. These extraordinary theories were, in part, an attempt to find a moral justification for the persecution of the misunderstood.

While men such as Aquinas were preaching their dire warnings to the faithful, an atmosphere of discreet homosexual tolerance had come to prevail in monasteries throughout Europe. That religious institutions provided a haven for homosexual men was one of the great ironies of medieval society. Even such future saints as the French St Anselm of Canterbury (1033–1109) and the English St Aelred of Rielvaux (1110–67) felt able to write of their amorous feelings for other men. Anselm, who became Archbishop of Canterbury in 1093, was bold enough to openly oppose the Council of London decrees that had attempted to punish any priests found guilty of sodomy. Anselm's near contemporary St Aelred was even less ambiguous in declaring his unashamed love for other men and acknowledging its physical expression in his relationship with his lover Simon, a monk.

Tacit acceptance of homosexual behaviour was also evident at the Court of the Holy Roman Emperor Charlemagne (774–814) at Aachen (in Germany today). Here, in AD 782 an English mathematician named Alcuin of York (735–804) arrived to become an advisor to the Emperor. His poems and letters, with their erotic passages and affectionate nicknames for his monk friends such as 'my little cuckoo', reveal Alcuin as a man of strong homosexual tendencies. Compared to the repressive St Peter Damian and the sanctimonious St Thomas Aquinas, Alcuin appears to have evoked the liberal world of the classical past. More accurately, however, he is an early harbinger of the Renaissance liberalism that was to come, encouraging Frankish scholars to explore the culture and beauty of ancient Greece and Rome.

The sexually liberal ideas of Alcuin and his disciples came to inspire the French clerical poets of the age, among them Baudri of Bourgueil (1046–1130) and his friend Marbod of Rennes (1035–1123). These men established a humanist circle in the Loire Valley, characterized by its sympathy for homosexual relationships. Among the English clerics attracted to this enlightened group was Serlo of Wilton (1105–81), who returned to his Cistercian monastery in England inspired by these new ideas. What these men shared was an undisguised admiration of male beauty in the old tradition of

Greek Love that had survived barbarian invasion and Christian persecution and remained a remarkable testimony to the power of natural emotion.

Belonging to a religious order gave men like Alcuin and Serlo considerable protection against a homophobic society but for a layman any accusation of sodomy could well prove fatal. Such a charge was later used to devastating effect in France to bring about the destruction of the most powerful order of chivalry in Europe, the Knights Templar. Resentful of the vast sums he owed them and of their power, fame and independence, Philip IV of France (1268-1314) decided to use homosexual scandal to overthrow them. Backed by Pope Clement V (1264-1314) he insisted that the Knights Templar were guilty of sodomy and must be totally suppressed, its leading members executed and its wealth passed to the French Crown. Only by combining the religious offence of blasphemy with the secular fear of homosexuality could the king's agents have hoped to mount a credible attack against such a respected institution as the Templars.

Elsewhere the first fully documented account of an execution for sodomy occurs in Germany in 1277, followed 15 years later by that of Adenolfo IV, Count of Acerra (d.1293), in southern Italy. Rooting out homosexuals now became a priority and where better to look for them than in the universities, where free thought and new, incendiary ideas had become dangerously prevalent. Intellectuals were thought to be the most dangerous disseminators of this heresy and in 1271 the English scholar Roger Bacon (c.1220-92) reported that many university lecturers in Paris had been involved in the practice and had been driven into exile as a result.

The 'problem' of homosexuality was now seen as so acute that its suppression was entrusted to the new proselytizing religious order of the Dominicans. In 1232, Pope Gregory IX (1145-1241) had commissioned them to eradicate heresy among the Cathar sect in southern France, a group also suspected of homosexual practices. The Dominicans later took control of the Holy Inquisition and acted ruthlessly, encouraging people to inform on homosexual suspects who were deemed heretics. Old scores could now be settled and rivals eliminated by simply denouncing them to the Inquisition.

Dominican power was later extended to the Spanish Inquisition, established in 1478. This offered little justice as the Inquisitor acted as both prosecutor and judge. In most cases the names of accusers and witnesses alike were withheld from the suspect, thus making any attempt at defence virtually impossible. Those accused were arrested, routinely tortured and then, having 'confessed', were sentenced to death. This ultimate penalty was known as 'relaxing', a euphemism for burning alive at the stake. Between 1570 and 1630 nearly 1,000 recorded sodomy trials took place before the Aragonese Inquisition in Spain and a further 500 under the jurisdiction of the Portuguese Inquisition. The result was that in 16th- and 17th-century Spain nearly as many people were executed for sodomy as for heresy.

As the 17th century progressed, the auto-da-fé processions gradually declined in number as the Inquisition realized that the shameful brutality involved reflected as much on its perpetrators as it did on the victims. Instead of burning alive, the convicted sodomite now faced enslavement in the galleys of Spain. There was also the growing suspicion that parading sodomites through the streets might be counterproductive as it could make the innocent curious to find out more about the sexual practices for which these men were being punished.

What was lost in this long, vicious and determined attempt to bully a minority into conformity was any consideration of the emotion that motivated same-sex relationships. For a religion that claimed to be based on universal love the Christian Church showed little tolerance of a form of love that lay outside its own rigid control. The devastation visited on gay people by the Holy Inquisition is one of the more extreme examples of this kind of horrific and seemingly senseless persecution. It affected even such nominally tolerant countries as Holland in the early 18th century, where a pogrom (massacre) against suspected sodomites was particularly vicious. Yet, there were those among the heterosexual majority in most societies who admired and protected those openly expressing same-sex love. Certainly, there was wide admiration among the English aristocracy in the late 18th century for Eleanor Butler (1739–1829) and Sarah Ponsonby (1755–1831), the Ladies of Llangollen (*see pages 61–68*). Their utter devotion to each other arguably put many heterosexual marriages to shame and, rather than being dismissed as pariahs, they became living national treasures and were visited by some of the most eminent people in the land, including William Wordsworth (1770–1850) and Sir Walter Scott (1771–1832).

But there were far more people quite willing, out of greed or vindictiveness, to accept police bribes and denounce the homosexuals or lesbians living among them in their communities. Where bribery failed, the authorities consistently used methods of entrapment to identify and punish gay people. The Nazi regime of the 1930s is one such example, but similar methods, including the infiltration of internet chat rooms, are still being used by Iran today.

One of the problems constantly faced by homosexuals has been the morbid fascination their lives have held for heterosexuals. For this reason there developed an obsession with the mechanics of same-sex relationships rather than an interest in their emotional content. Even the constant use in law of the words 'sodomy' and 'buggery' were indicative of the need to dismiss emotions that many found hard to understand. Appropriately both terms are completely and historically false, for it is now universally acknowledged that the sin leading to the destruction of the city of Sodom in the Old Testament was not anal intercourse but either idolatry or a lack of hospitality. The same misappropriation is true of buggery, which is, in fact, a corruption of the name of a small religious sect in ancient Bulgaria that was opposed by the Christian Church.

One of the great disappointments of history is that most contemporary accounts are so unrevealing, telling us little of the thoughts or vulnerabilities of the people who wrote them. When it comes to emotion and, above all, personal sexuality virtually nothing exists other than the boastful accounts of Benvenuto Cellini's bisexual adventures in Renaissance Florence or Giacomo Casanova's (1725–98) long list of heterosexual conquests a century later. Only in the late 18th and early 19th centuries do writers and diarists begin to openly record the details of their sex lives, both hetero and homo.

The reason for such reticence is understandable, for recording such personal details could prove dangerous. Not only was sodomy a serious crime punishable by death, exile or imprisonment but the very mention of it shocked conventional society. Lord Byron's exile from England, for example, was brought about not by the common knowledge of his adulterous affairs but by his homoerotic correspondence being revealed to the press. Exile and social disgrace were also the price that the wealthy William Beckford (1760–1844), Byron's near contemporary, had to pay when the contents of his love letters to a young male cousin were discovered. That people such as the writer Anne Lister (1791–1840) and William Beckford in the 18th century were brave enough to record their own homoerotic emotions is a tribute to their honesty and courage.

Even in the 19th century, men with strong homosexual tendencies, such as the writers Edward Lear (1812–88) and Henry James (1843–1916), were terrified to record their true emotions, preferring to remain safely in the closet. Only such brave and pioneering souls as Edward Carpenter (1844–1929) and A. J. Symonds had the courage to write or attempt to publish open and unapologetic accounts of their homosexual lives. Few of their contemporaries were prepared to be as bold. Having written in praise of male comradeship and bonding in *Leaves of Grass* (1855), the American poet Walt Whitman (1819–92) then took fright and went to great lengths to deny his homosexuality, even to other sympathetic men.

Well into the 20th century the risk of scandal hung over anyone prepared to openly discuss homosexuality. When, in 1928, the English writer Marguerite Radclyffe Hall (1880–1943) published her novel of lesbian love, *The Well of Loneliness*, it caused a scandal and the author was prosecuted for obscenity on the basis of a single phrase '*and that night, they were not divided*'.

Something must now be said about the terms used in this book to refer to same-sex love. It would have been inappropriate to apply the term 'gay' to those involved in such relationships before the 18th century. The first appearance of 'gay' in its modern sense was in press reports of the young male prostitutes involved in London's notorious Cleveland Street Scandal of 1889. Only after 1971 has the word become the standard reference to describe homosexuality and it would have been meaningless to Henry James and his contemporaries in the 19th century. For this reason I have generally used the term 'homosexual' throughout and have phased in the word 'gay' when it seemed historically appropriate.

The use of 'gay' in a lesbian context is even more recent, probably first occurring in *Miss Furr & Miss Skeene* (1922) by Gertrude Stein (1874–1946). Less of a problem exists with the word 'lesbian', which has been used consistently since the 17th century together with its alternative, 'Sapphist' (referring to people who followed Sappho's lifestyle).

Perhaps the current, almost universal, acceptance of the word 'gay' in Western society suggests that the long period of persecution and exile for homosexuals is finally over. Perhaps we are witnessing, if not a return to the values of ancient Greece, then at least a willingness to encourage gay people to play a fully integrated role in modern society. For those people driven into exile such as Lord Byron (*see pages 69–78*) or those who chose exile such as the writer Paul Bowles (*see pages 165–74*), their achievements remain as a testament to their pioneering spirit and this book hopefully shows that. Their lives are certainly a testament to the words of Ralph Waldo Emerson: 'Do not follow where the path may lead. Go, instead, where there is no path and leave a trail.'

MIGNONS AND LIBERTINES

The homosexual artists of the Renaissance in Italy may have found an accommodation, if not open tolerance, from the Catholic Church but elsewhere in Europe it was a far different matter. Italy's reputation as the 'home of sodomy' was given further credence in Protestant eyes when Julius III (1487–1555) became Pope in 1551. The presiding figure at the Council of Trent six years earlier, Julius had shown little zeal in enforcing its condemnation of sodomy. Instead, he spent much of his time with his attractive favourite, the 15-year-old, Innocenzo, who he made a cardinal. This was seen throughout Europe as an outrageous combination of nepotism and sexual depravity that deeply shocked Catholics and provided their enemies with invaluable ammunition. Protestant polemicists eager for an onslaught on sexual deviants set about attacking Julius III with relish, one Thomas Beard calling him a 'lustful satyr' who was determined 'to promote none to ecclesiastical livings save only his buggers.' Another critic, the Swiss Protestant Thomas Erastus (1524–83), described Julius as waiting at a window in the Vatican for Innocenzo to arrive 'with all the impatience of a man whose mistress had promised him a night.' Faced with this serious embarrassment Catholic theologians responded by pointing out that John Calvin's (1509–64) French assistant, Théodore de Bèze (1519–1605), had been the author of numerous homoerotic Latin verses, including one in which a man debates the choice between his male and female lover.

Protestants in general, and Calvinists in particular, had rejected the Roman Catholic belief that sex should be for the purpose of procreation in marriage alone. Now, in the ascendancy, they became even more fanatic than Catholics in rooting out the evil of homosexual intercourse, while at the same time promoting the domestic joys of married intercourse. The centre of Calvinism was the Swiss city of Geneva, where a theocracy based upon Old Testament teachings had been established in 1535. While there had been only a handful of sodomy trials prior to the arrival of Calvin, there were 60 in just over a century after Geneva became Calvinist. Of these, 30 ended in conviction and the guilty were executed by burning, hanging, drowning and beheading. Particularly brutal was the treatment of a prominent Geneva official Pierre Canal, who confessed under torture to being a homosexual and implicated more than 20 other men. Canal was broken on the wheel for treason and then burned alive for sodomy. Of those named by Canal, three men were drowned and the rest sent into exile. What is extraordinary about the Geneva persecutions is that those put to death in a city of just 12,000 inhabitants exceeded in proportion those executed in Spain by the Inquisition.

The persecution reached a climax in the 1560s, when Théodore de Bèze (1519–1605), presumably having abandoned his own interest in same sex-relations, presided over a Geneva that was fast becoming the refuge for many French Protestants escaping Catholic intolerance elsewhere. The records show that six French and one Italian immigrant were banished for sodomy while another four Frenchmen were drowned for the same crime.

The one reported case of lesbianism in Geneva gave the authorities a difficult task in deciding the sentence as there was no precedent for such a crime. Reference was made to the Carolina Code of neighbouring Germany, named in honour of the Emperor Charles V (1500–58; Holy Roman Emperor 1519–56). This ordained the penalties for many sexual offences, including execution by burning for 'anyone committing impurity with a beast, or a man with a man, or a *woman with a woman.*' Wherever the empire ruled, the Carolina Code was used to morally and legally control the people. Even captives taken in war did not escape its harsh penalties and 30 Turks captured by Imperial forces were first tortured to force confessions of sodomy before being burned alive. The Carolina was also used in the Low Countries, along with the Spanish Inquisition, to maintain control in an area of mixed religion. When

Protestants gained control of Bruges and Ghent, revenge was taken and a large number of Catholic Franciscans and Augustinians were accused and convicted of sodomy and burned at the stake.

In the midst of this religious persecution, thinly disguised as a crusade against sexual immorality, France had the good fortune to be a relative oasis of tolerance. Henry III (1551–89; King of France 1575–89) was a curious combination of action man and sensitive aesthete. As an 18-year-old soldier, he had led the Catholic forces to victory against the Protestant Huguenots at the Battle of Jarnac in 1569. This success led to his election as King of Poland in 1573 and, while in Warsaw, he was said to have been initiated into homosexual practices by René de Villequier. One of Henry's accompanying courtiers, René 'imbued him with the vice which nature detests which he could not unlearn'. When his brother Charles IX died in 1574, Henry returned to France as king and from the moment of his arrival abandoned military interests, in favour of making the French court a centre of culture. Henry surrounded himself, like a latter-day Nero, with his *mignons* – handsome and athletic young men described by the chronicler Pierre de l'Estoile as wearing 'velvet bonnets like the whores in the brothels'. He also caustically described how the group got its name:

> *The name 'Mignons' began, at this time, to travel by word of mouth among the people, to whom they were very odious, as much for their mocking and haughty ways as for their made-up faces and effeminate clothes ... they gamble, blaspheme and fornicate following the King everywhere ... seeking to please him in everything they do and say, caring little for God or virtue.*

Among Henry's favourite *mignons* were François d'Espinay, who had accompanied him to Poland and was rewarded with the Château of Rozoy-en-Brie and the governorship of Brouage; Anne, Duc de Joyeuse, and Jean Louis de Nogaret de la Valette, Duc d'Épernon.

Such outrageous behaviour served only to provoke the anger and condemnation of the more conservative members of both the Church and the aristocracy. Combining indolence with bouts of feverish activity, Henry would often appear in feminine clothes with his face made up and wearing elaborate necklaces. His handsome young friends were equally flamboyant and Henry lavished wealth and attention on them, often addressing them by feminine nicknames. Among his bitterest critics were the Protestant Huguenots, whose destruction in the St Bartholomew's Day Massacre of 1572 Henry had encouraged. One of them, the poet Agrippa d'Aubigné (1552–1630), constantly mocked the sovereign's suspected taste for passive homosexuality by describing him as 'a King–Man or more accurately, a Man–Queen.' D'Aubigné attributed the king's disinterest in the military affairs that had occupied his youth to his homosexuality. The fact that he was married meant little in an age when many of the leading military commanders in Europe were bisexual.

Traditional Catholics were equally critical of Henry's tolerance of sexual deviation, particularly after it became apparent that if his remaining brother died childless then the heir to the French throne would be the Protestant Prince Henry of Navarre (1553–1610; King of France 1589–1610). A vitriolic campaign against the king began with accusations of tyranny, heresy, sorcery and, equally damaging to his moral reputation with his contemporaries, sodomy. Accusations of this and other sins appeared in almost 1,000 pamphlets distributed throughout France at the time. Dark allusions were made to the fate suffered by Edward II (1284–1327; King of England 1307–27) when he refused to abandon his own favourites – a red hot poker was inserted into his entrails ... Henry's *mignons* were attacked as being either political thugs or royal bedfellows, provoking skirmishes between them and the supporters of the Catholic Duc of Guise. When two of his favourite mignons were killed in a brawl, Henry commissioned a statue to commemorate them, just as the Athenians had done for Harmodius and Aristogiton. This gesture infuriated the Paris mob and in 1588 it attacked and destroyed the monument.

The mignons were seen as part of a larger group of immoralists known as 'Libertines', who were bent on destroying traditional beliefs and morals. In 1605 they were attacked in a book entitled *The*

Hermaphrodites, which claimed to reveal their secret, evil world and mocked their penchant for bright jewels and elegant clothes. More dangerously, it equated sexual deviation with social, political and cultural treachery. It was another significant addition to the armoury of those who sought to portray homosexuality as a threat to society. Such works helped to provoke renewed opposition to Henry, as many considered that through his depraved lifestyle he had surrendered his divine right to rule France as king. It was not perhaps surprising when, on 1 August 1589, Henry was attacked and stabbed to death by a fanatical Dominican monk.

His successor, Henry of Navarre, was as sexually active as his predecessor but restricted himself to conventional heterosexuality. As Henry IV, he inaugurated a new era of religious tolerance. His realistic attitude to religion and eagerness to compromise was perfectly expressed in his famous saying 'Paris is well worth a mass.' Under Navarre's rule, free speech was encouraged and open debate returned to the universities. Henry III's *mignons* disappeared and were replaced by the Libertines as the object of public ridicule. These were essentially sybarites dedicated to the enjoyment of pleasure in a society that had endured a grim period of religious intolerance. The Libertines' philosophy was based on the truism that since God had created everything then nothing, not even homosexuality, should be considered sinful. What annoyed traditionalists most, however, was not their flamboyant appearance but the suspicion that they denied the immortality of the soul and were heavily involved in demonology and witchcraft. The Libertines were clearly recognized by their elaborate dress. One contemporary writer, Pierre L'Estoile, condemned

> ... *those miserable, effeminate ones, bearded women who know neither virtue nor courage. They prance down the street with their hair curled like hermaphrodites. Their main concern is to stuff their guts with delicacies.*

Here is evidence of a popular contemporary belief that diet could determine sexuality. Overindulgence in general was assumed to be the cause of deviant behaviour throughout Europe. In England the great jurist Sir Edward Coke (1552–1634) blamed contemporary homosexuality on 'pride, excess of diet, idleness and contempt of the poor'.

One of the most outrageous of the French Libertines was the poet Théophile de Viau (1590–1626), whose iconoclastic ideas and outrageous lifestyle had much in common with the English poet and Libertine sympathizer, the bisexual John Wilmot, Earl of Rochester (1647–80). A celebrated figure at the court of Charles II (1630–85; King of Great Britain and Ireland 1660–85), Rochester was a friend of de Viau and, like him, challenged prevailing social conventions. Rochester's sexual escapades and his obscene and satirical poetry led to the king repeatedly exiling him from court. In one of his most provocative poems 'Love a Woman? You're an Ass!', Rochester mocks heterosexual love as 'designed for dirty slaves' and contrasts it to more rewarding homosexual relations. The striking difference between Rochester and de Viau, however, was Rochester's willingness to apologize when having caused offence. This, together with his high social standing which offered him powerful royal protection, saved Rochester from the fate that befell Théophile de Viau.

Born in 1590 at Clairac into a Huguenot family who had recently been promoted to the ranks of the lesser nobility, de Viau studied medicine in Bordeaux and Holland, before joining a troupe of travelling actors for whom he wrote plays. A charming and handsome man, de Viau became the most popular and successful poet of the age, publishing five times the amount of verse produced by his better-known contemporary François de Malherbe (1555–1628).

As the most celebrated Libertine author of the age, de Viau advocated the idea that a man should look to nature for moral guidance rather than to the Church, and follow his own natural instincts. Such a Libertarian concept brought de Viau great notoriety and considerable sympathy from ordinary men forbidden the sexual freedom traditionally enjoyed by the aristocracy. In this sense the fastidious de Viau was a genuine man of the people, writing in simple and often salacious language that allowed his poems to be read in taverns rather than in the grand literary salons of the age. His subject matter also appealed to the powerless and dispossessed because it mocked the hypocrisy and corruption of both the Huguenot and Roman Catholic churches. With such powerful bodies united against him, de Viau found few members of the laity bold enough to defend his personal campaign for free speech. Finally, in 1619, de Viau's many enemies among the clergy united to force the King to exile him from France.

In England he found a court that bore remarkable similarity to that of the late Henry III of France. James I (1566–1625; King of England 1603–25 and James VI of Scotland 1567–1625) was as equally cultivated as his fellow monarch and similarly drawn to his own 'mignons', a series of male lovers whose interests he defended against the rest of the aristocracy. Openly homosexual, James I managed a display of moral hypocrisy seldom rivalled in history. He even reviewed the Buggery Act of 1533, imposed by Henry VIII (1491–1547; King of England 1509–47), making it even harsher and describing sodomy as one of those horrible crimes that 'ye are bound in conscience never to forgive.' In his treatise on government, the 'Basilikon Doron', James described sodomy as an offence that should never be pardoned and in 1610 refused to pardon those convicted of it. Clearly this moral rectitude was not meant to apply to kings for James's first lover, when he was King of Scotland, had been Esmé Stuart, Duke of Lennox (1542–83), who James was given to kissing openly in public. Such behaviour scandalized the Scottish Kirk and nobility who united in having Lennox banished to France. Lennox was replaced in James's affections by Robert Carr, Earl of Somerset (1590–1645), who was appropriately appointed the Gentleman of the Bedchamber. The bisexual Carr eventually decided that he preferred to marry wealthy heiress Frances Howard (1590–1632) and ended the relationship with the King, who moved on to the charming and handsome George Villiers, Duke of Buckingham (1592–1628).

When Théophile de Viau arrived in London, he became acquainted with Buckingham. Both were cynics, who had depended on royal protection to survive, although in de Viau's case even the

King of France could not withstand the combined pressure of the Huguenot and Roman Catholic church. De Viau must have known the intimate details of the relationship, for he wrote a scurrilous and widely circulated verse about 'Apollo with his songs debauched young Hyacinthus / And it is well known that the King of England / F***s the Duke of Buckingham'.

After little more than a year of exile in England, de Viau was allowed to return to France on condition that he avoid Paris and remain at his family estate at Boussères de Mazeres in Aquitaine. Dangerously isolated by his insistence on belonging to no party or faction, he wisely rethought his position and decided to nominally convert to Catholicism. Such a free spirit could not be repressed for long, however, and he defiantly translated Plato's *Treatise on the Immortality of the Soul* and began composing his most famous and controversial work, *The Satirical Parnassus*, which contained some licentious poems. When it appeared in 1623, the book immediately caught the attention of Jesuit Father François Garasse (1585–1631). He denounced de Viau as the ringleader of a band of dangerous atheists and sodomites who were in 'the vanguard of the Antichrist'. Summoned to appear before the ecclesiastical court in Paris and face charges of *lèse-majesté divine* (insulting the sovereign) and of writing atheistic poems advocating sodomy, de Viau sensibly failed to materialize, having gone into hiding. The dangers he faced were all too real: four years earlier, a man of similar disposition to de Viau, the Italian philosopher Lucilio Vanini (1585–1619), had been pursued by the Jesuits for blasphemy. He had his tongue cut out and was burned alive in Toulouse.

Deprived of its prey, the court ordered that de Viau be burned in effigy instead outside Notre Dame. On the run and intending to escape to England, de Viau was caught before he could reach Calais and was taken back to Paris where he was imprisoned in the Conciergerie, where Marie Antoinette had been held. From there, de Viau addressed a poem to his lover and fellow poet Jacques la Vallée des Barreaux (1599–1673), lamenting that he had done nothing to help de Viau. The realization that he was now beyond the help of even his closest friends provoked such despair that de Viau began to contemplate suicide. Yet, while incarcerated in the Conciergerie, de Viau's persecution had become a cause célèbre throughout Europe. Scholars were outraged at the cruel treatment he had received for his defence of free speech. That he had been charged under archaic laws relating to blasphemy was almost as shocking for men who had witnessed the bloody results of religious bigotry.

The campaign to have de Viau freed was taken to be one of the first signs of the coming Enlightenment, when reason not religion became the basis of philosophy. A furious debate over what defined free speech and what was meant by blasphemy began. Over 50 pamphlets concerning the de Viau affair were published in the course of this heated discussion, the great majority supporting his case and calling for his freedom. Such united support for an individual and his right to pursue his own ideas, no matter how controversial, had never been seen in France before and Henry of Navarre was forced to recognize the clamour for mercy. The death sentence was grudgingly commuted to that of permanent exile from the kingdom of France.

Yet, the controversy had gained de Viau a new friend and powerful protector in the person of the Duke of Montmorency, who brought pressure to bear for a retrial and demanded a full inquiry into the reasons for de Viau's original conviction. With spirits restored, de Viau claimed that his accusers were liars and hypocrites. At the hearing he sensationally claimed that he had personally caught the prosecutor, Father Voisin, in flagrante with the main witness, a young Jesuit named Louis Sageot. At this Sageot broke down and admitted that he had lied and perjured himself at the behest of Voisin and des Barreaux stood up in court, claiming that Voisin had tried to seduce him, too, when he was a student at the same Jesuit college.

The hearing ended in turmoil with de Viau vindicated and the Jesuits mocked as hypocrites and liars. The whole affair had become an embarrassing scandal for France. Although de Viau had been wrongfully perjured, he had admitted his own homosexuality. The final verdict was that Théophile de Viau should be sent into exile from France but that the perjurer, Father Voisin, should also be banished, so demonstrating the even-handed justice of Henry IV. The honesty and openness that de Viau had demonstrated gained him many sympathizers and he had become so popular that his banishment was not enforced. There were conditions, however, and de Viau had to keep a low profile, stay out of Paris and avoid further controversy.

Eventually, at the request of his most important supporter, the King's favourite, the Duc de Luyne (1578-1621), de Viau was quietly allowed to return to Paris and even to attend Court, where he won new fame as a poet. Théophile's poetry appeared unaffected by its author's tribulations and its celebration of physical beauty and all the pleasures of life made his poetry extremely popular. Some 88 editions of his work appeared between 1621 and 1696 making him the most published poet in 17th-century France.

Throughout his long ordeal, de Viau had been sustained by the belief that freedom of thought and expression were the most precious legacies of the Renaissance that must be preserved at all cost. Above all, a man should spend his limited time on Earth enjoying the pleasures of existence and live 'in a spirit of generosity'. Théophile's ideas derived from the Epicurean philosophy of Greece and Rome, as expressed in the work of Lucretius (flourished 1st century BC), Horace (65-8 BC), Pliny (the Elder, AD 23-79) and Seneca (4 BC–AD 65), and more recently, Giulio Vanini. Each of these men had been Libertine in spirit and followers of natural law but the ideas they produced presented a powerful challenge to the moral dictatorship of the Christian Church. Freedom of speech was one thing, but the promotion of homosexuality quite another. De Viau's open relationships with other men made him an obvious target. His enemy, Father Garasse, had bitterly condemned the group of writers and young aristocrats drawn to de Viau as the 'the free spirits' suggesting that their sexual behaviour was just as uncontrolled as their thinking. Certainly, de Viau made little attempt to disguise his approval of all male relationships, including his own with Jacques la Vallée des Barreaux. After his lover's death, de Viau was mockingly referred to as des Barreaux's 'widow'.

When de Viau died in 1626, Henry of Navarre's successor, Louis XIII (1601–43; King of France 1610–43) had been on the French throne for 16 years. As much a homosexual as Henry III had been, Louis had neither his predecessor's effeminacy nor his attachment to mignons, preferring hunting and warfare to cross-dressing.

Deprived of love as a young child and having seen his mother, Marie de Medici (1573-1642), driven into exile, Louis turned to his servants for affection, including his coachman, his falconer and dog keeper. At the age of 10, he developed a passion for the Duc de Luynes, Théophile de Viau's protector and his late father's favourite, preferring his company to that of his child bride, Anne of Austria (1601–66). After de Luynes died, the morose monarch largely left the administration of France to Cardinal Richelieu (1585–1642), while consoling himself with a series of relationships with attractive young men, such as his equerry François de Baradas. Later in life, he became obsessed with the stylish and handsome Marquis de Cinq Mars (1620–42), a protégé of Cardinal Richelieu. One courtier recorded entering Cinq Mars's room, where he was anointing himself with jasmine oil in preparation for a visit from the king. Misjudging the hold he had over the king, Cinq Mars brought about his own sudden end by plotting a coup with the king's brother. Nothing could save him, least of all his lover, and Cinq Mars was beheaded at Lyon.

The legacy of Théophile de Viau and the Libertines, if not that of Louis XIII, survived long after their deaths into the new age of the Enlightenment, as did their insistence that sexuality was a personal matter and that homosexual relationships should be tolerated, even if not sanctioned by the Church. Homosexuality in France had become irrevocably associated with the Court and the debauched aristocracy and the fear among the clergy was that it was spreading insidiously throughout society. An early biographer of the new king, Louis XIV (1638–1715; King of France 1643–1715), lamented 'the beau vice' that had once been the exclusive preserve of noblemen and men of wit and fashion was now prevalent among the people in general. He urged the young king to take firm action to stop the moral rot before it was too late. The message was not wasted on the 5-year-old king's advisors, who swiftly issued a decree in his name exiling a group of young aristocrats from the country for holding a party for homosexuals in the gardens of Versailles. Many at the time would have thought exile from Versailles punishment enough, for the palace was then the centre of the French universe. This action indicated a change in the moral climate that would in future be governed, not by the Church, but by the civil authorities in the name of the king. To protect the young from homosexual contamination, the Paris police began to take an interest in well known aristocratic homosexuals. One of them was the elderly Duc de la Battue, who was notorious for his obsession with young boys. Unless he mended his ways, he was told, he would either be exiled or end up in the St Lazare prison. Others thought to be corrupting the young were incarcerated at the Hospital General at Bicêtre, south of Paris, where, in the manner of an English debtors' prison, they could pay for better food and more comfortable rooms. Consistent good behaviour earned early release and in times of war the miscreant could earn pardon by enlisting in the army. The extreme barbarities of the previous century had gone, but the new punishment was certainly not lenient and included deportation to the French West Indies along with the more persistent female prostitutes rounded up in Paris.

Yet, de Viau's influence on later thinkers was far in excess of his merits as a poet. His personal crusade for intellectual freedom would win him many admirers centuries after his death. When the French philosopher Simone Weil (1909–43), went into exile to escape the German occupation of France in 1942, she took with her a copy of his poems. What appealed most to the neurotic but highly principled Weil was de Viau's irrepressible spirit. Weil's interest in a man, whose work had been neglected for the past two centuries, was significant because, like her, de Viau refused to conform. In many ways his life paralleled that of Oscar Wilde (*see pages 107–118*) and it was no coincidence that the man chosen to edit the first modern edition of de Viau's poems was another iconoclast, the bisexual André Gide (1869–1951), who in his youth had been a friend of Wilde's during his last days in Paris.

THE FLIGHT OF QUEEN CHRISTINA

When Théophile de Viau was still a child, the Abbé de Brantôme (1540–1614), once a soldier and courtier but now a Catholic priest, was writing his memoirs and completing *The Lives of Gallant Ladies*, the first modern book to deal seriously with lesbianism.

After a lifetime spent at the French court, Brantôme was intrigued by the contradictions and complexities of human sexuality. More a Libertine in spirit than a priest, Brantôme dealt so dispassionately with the subject of male and female homosexuality that his book can arguably be seen as the first objective work of sexology in history.

What fascinated Brantôme more was lesbianism, of which he wrote approvingly, and he was the first person to use the term in its modern sense. Brantôme was convinced that lesbianism had a single cause – the absence of men. When husbands went off to war or travelled away from home, women turned to each other for emotional support and sexual relief. When the man returned, the woman resumed her heterosexual relationship. This was essentially the same argument in reverse, used to explain the bisexuality of many sailors. For a Catholic priest writing in the 17th century, Brantôme's ideas were extraordinarily liberal: he considered lesbianism morally superior to the only alternative, infidelity. When involved in a same-sex relationship, a woman was not cuckolding her husband nor risking the dangers of pregnancy or abortion – thus, lesbianism was a form of safe sex.

There is little doubt that Brantôme's radical approach to sexuality was encouraged by the classical literature of Greece and Rome that had reappeared during the Renaissance. Among these rediscoveries were the poems of the Greek poet Sappho, with their passionate declarations of female love, which appeared in French for the first time. Others beside the Abbé de Brantôme were won over by their lyrical beauty. The scholar Tanneguy Le Fèvre (1615–72), a protégé of Cardinal Richelieu, wrote coyly, if approvingly of Sappho in his *Lives of the Greek Poets*, describing her as having 'an amorous disposition but unsatisfied by that which other women find in the company of men ... she wanted mistresses of her own.' This interest in lesbianism was highly disapproved of by some of his fellow academicians and Le Fèvre was dismissed from his post at the Academy of Saumur.

While lesbianism had largely been ignored in the past, it was suddenly made public by one of the most controversial and enigmatic monarchs in European history, Queen Christina of Sweden. Her birth in 1626 was an extraordinary event as the entire court was expecting a boy to succeed to the Swedish throne.

Hiding his disappointment at her sex, her father Gustav Adolf (1594–1632; King of Sweden 1611–32) resolved to treat her in every respect as a boy. When Gustav was killed at the Battle of Lutzen in 1632, the six-year-old Christina came to the throne and her education continued in accordance with her father's wishes. She was given toy soldiers to play with rather than dolls and, in the manner of Elizabeth I of England (1533–1603; Queen of England 1558–1603), was taught by the most distinguished scholars, among them the internationally respected Dr Matthiæ, Bishop of Strengès. Like Elizabeth I, Christina proved to be a dedicated student who, by the age of 10, was one of the best educated royals in Europe. Not surprisingly given her early indoctrination into all things male, she appeared to have little or no interest in traditionally feminine pursuits or amusements. For the rest of her life Christina dressed as a man, shunning long dresses and jewellery.

A comparable female cross-dresser in Europe at the time was Margaret Cavendish, the Duchess of Newcastle (1623–73), who wore a mixture of male and female clothes and greeted her guests with a masculine bow. A talented writer, the Duchess had penned a work provocatively entitled *The Convent of Pleasure*, in which women shun men and enjoy passionate relationships together.

Without the responsibilities of state that would weigh so heavily on Christina, the Duchess found the time to publish 14 volumes of poetry, prose, plays and a biography of her husband, plus five volumes of natural philosophy. Finding little support from other women for her ideas, she came to believe that marriage undermines the psychological independence necessary for female achievement.

In Queen Christina's case the cross-dressing was not an erotic ploy intended to provoke men, but the consequence of her obvious desire to act and appear like a man, perhaps resulting from her unusual upbringing. This was in complete contrast to Elizabeth I of England, who while keeping a virginal distance from men, often used her sex appeal as a useful tool when dealing with foreign diplomats. The extraordinary account of an audience with the French ambassador Monsieur de Maisse is testimony to this:

> *She kept the front of her dress open and one could see the whole of her bosom, when she raises her head she has a trick of putting both hands on her gown and opening it so that her belly can be seen.*

Such an obviously feminine ploy would have been anathema to Christina, whose dress and demeanour continued to appall her mother Marie Eleanora of Brandenburg (1599–1655), who pleaded with her daughter to show greater femininity in her behaviour. This was to prove impossible for a woman who walked and rode a horse like a man and whose voice was deep and gruff. She was to all intents a man trapped in a woman's body.

Christina's characteristically masculine behaviour may have been rare at the time but it was certainly not unique. Her French contemporary, Catherine de la Guette, considered herself possessed of a similar 'warrior' temperament. Like Christina, Catherine's father had taught her military skills so that she could defend their estate during the French civil wars known as the Fronde (1648–1653). Dressed as a soldier Catherine abandoned her music and embroidery and fought on horseback alongside the men from her estate. Again like Christina, she was rumoured to be attracted to women and to have pursued an affair with at least one local girl.

When Christina's aunt died, her role of nominal guardian passed to the sister of the Swedish Chancellor, Axel Oxenstierna (1583-1654). He was a highly experienced soldier and diplomat who was to have the greatest influence on the young Queen's intellectual development. Under his tutelage, Christina made even greater progress in her preparation for taking control of Swedish affairs. Oxenstierna was as perplexed as everyone else by her masculinity, although he paid her a backhanded compliment by saying, 'she is not at all like a woman ... but possessed of a bright intelligence'.

Working 12 hours a day at her studies, Christina soon mastered French, German and Italian, as well as gaining a good working knowledge of Flemish, Spanish and Latin. Her grasp of ancient history, art, music and the sciences was also exceptional for a woman of her times. Up until the age of 18, she had ruled Sweden under a regency but, in December 1644, she assumed full control of the nation. She dedicated herself to affairs of state with the same enthusiasm that she had already applied to her education, swiftly concluding peace negotiations with Sweden's adversary, Denmark.

Obsessed by French culture, Christina established a reputation as a polymath, a patron of the arts and as a true progenitor of the 18th Enlightenment – the European intellectual movement of the 17th and 18th centuries that pursued the use and celebration of knowledge, freedom and happiness. She established a French ballet-troupe under Antoine de Beaulieu in 1638 and brought Italian and French orchestras to court. An amateur actress herself, drama flourished in Christina's court and her court poet, Georg Stiernhielm, wrote several plays in Swedish for Christina.

This cultural initiative was all the more surprising given that Sweden was looked upon as one of the most culturally backward of European countries. Keenly aware of this, Christina strove to improve her country's self-esteem by encouraging it to develop its educational and economic potential. She set about attracting some of the greatest minds in Europe to Stockholm, men such as the eminent philosopher René Descartes (1596–1650), the educationalist John Comenius (1592–1670) and the Dutch lawyer Hugo Grotius (1583–1645). Although the financial rewards were attractive, the infamous Swedish climate led some scholars to politely refuse the Queen's invitation.

With her own growing confidence and the presence and advice of such wise and talented men, Christina began developing a more internationalist and open-minded approach to diplomacy. Her decisive intervention in the negotiations to end the Thirty Years' War (1618–48) in the Treaty of Westphalia, signed at Osnabruck, for example, earned her international gratitude and admiration.

Just as a golden age of peace, prosperity and international esteem appeared imminent for Sweden, a wholly unexpected crisis concerning Christina's sexuality and religious beliefs arose. From childhood it had been assumed that the Queen would eventually marry and produce an heir. At 16, she had even thought herself in love with her cousin, Charles Gustav (1622–60; King of Sweden 1654–60), and like Elizabeth I of England, she constantly flirted with many of the younger diplomats at Court, yet, there it ended. As time passed Christina became increasingly convinced that she could never marry any man, writing that 'she felt so great a repulsion towards the marital state that she would rather choose death than a man'. She even told the French ambassador that she could never submit her body to a man for it would mean being 'treated like a field in which a peasant plants his seeds'. These are unambiguous statements of physical revulsion at heterosexual contact, but do not necessarily mean that Christina was lesbian. What is certain is that her views on sex were distinctly Libertine for the conservative Sweden of her time. Nor did she hesitate in offering her opinion on sexual matters, once shocking the court by openly defending homosexuality.

It is not surprising that both Christina's attitudes and appearance alarmed her Swedish subjects just as much as it surprised such visiting foreign dignitaries as Oliver Cromwell's secretary of state, John Thurloe (1616–68), who reported back to London that 'nature is mistaken in her and that she was intended for a man'.

Christina's sexual ambiguity had become a constant subject of discussion at court but a rumour that she had become pregnant by her French physician, Pierre Bourdelot, was no more convincing than the story that she had forced a visiting French countess 'to perform immoral acts' on her.

In both Sweden and France the Queen's opponents had decided that sexual innuendo was the best means of damaging a royal reputation. More convincing proof of Christina's lesbian sympathy was her open and passionate love for one of her own ladies-in-waiting, Countess Ebba Sparre. The affair began soon after Christina came to the throne and is confirmed by the series of unequivocal love letters that Christina wrote to Ebba. Such emotional correspondence between high-born women in the 17th century was not unusual, nor was the fact that Christina and Ebba often shared a bed together. Contemporary witnesses, however, had no doubt that the relationship was as physical as it was emotional. The Danish ambassador reported that Christina had 'hidden the beautiful Ebba Sparre in her bed and associated with her in a special way'.

In the 17th century, lesbianism was still a mystery to most men and of little concern for the moralists, who thought that if such strange activity between women did exist then it would surely be confined to the Catholic convents, where it presented no threat to male sexual supremacy. This view was commonly held throughout Europe and even the Dutch theologian Erasmus (1469–1536) wrote knowingly 'not everything among the virgins is virginal because there are more who copy Sappho's behaviour than share her talent'.

At the same time as she was struggling with her lesbian emotions Christina was developing a profound and – for a Swedish queen – dangerous interest in Roman Catholicism. When the Vatican heard of this, Pope Alexander VII (1599–1667) discreetly encouraged Antonio Macedo, a Jesuit priest posing as the

Portuguese ambassador's interpreter, to pursue the matter. Macedo arranged for two learned Jesuit professors, Fathers Malines and Casati, to travel incognito, posing as Italian noblemen, and begin working at court. They later reported that Christina was utterly sincere in her desire to embrace Catholicism. As the time for her conversion approached, all concerned were sworn to the utmost secrecy and it may well be that the two Jesuits carried out the ceremony as early as 1652, more than a year before she admitted her change of religion and abdicated the throne.

When her decision to become a Catholic was made public it astonished the whole of Europe – Protestant and Catholic alike – and shocked the ordinary Swedish people far more than any rumours of their sovereign's sexual irregularity that might have filtered down to them from court gossip. Without doubt it was the most famous religious conversion since that of the Emperor Constantine to Christianity in AD 312.

As a Catholic Christina could not possibly continue to rule Protestant Sweden and a constitutional crisis was inevitable. Her reasons for converting were discussed everywhere, although few saw it as connected with her personal sexual dilemma. Had she remained queen, the pressure to marry a man and produce an heir to the Swedish throne would have been intense, yet she had also increasingly found the idea of carnality unbearable. Only by leaving the country altogether could she avoid this childbearing responsibility and find personal freedom. Her conversion to Catholicism, no matter how genuine in spirit, might well have provided her with a solution to this problem. Therefore on 6 June 1654, Queen Christina formally abdicated the Swedish throne in favour of her cousin, Charles Gustav, the man whom she had once thought of marrying. During the abdication ceremony at Uppsala castle, Christina wore her full regalia, which was removed from her, one piece at a time. To celebrate her newfound freedom, she cut her hair shorter than it had ever been in her life and, with a new confidence, put on men's clothes. Her only regret on leaving Sweden, she said, was that she had been unable to persuade Ebba to accompany her.

In early November 1655, Christina was formally received into the Catholic Church. Christina's arrival in Rome was a triumph for Pope Alexander VII and for several months she was the sole preoccupation of the Pope and his court. Roman nobles vied with each other to entertain her, offering endless displays of fireworks, jousts, fake combats, acrobatics and operas. At the Palazzo Aldobrandini she was welcomed by a crowd of 6,000 spectators and watched an amazing procession of camels and elephants. In Sweden, however, her people were far from content. Not only had their Queen become a Catholic, but she had done it at the very heart of Catholicism and in a dramatic ceremony involving the Pope himself. To most Protestants this was a monumental and unprecedented act of temporal and spiritual betrayal. At a time of bitter, protracted religious wars, in which Lutheran Sweden had for 30 years fought constantly against the Catholic empire, such a conversion seemed more like capitulation to the enemy rather than a personal act of conscience.

Christina began her new life in Rome free of the pressures that had surrounded her in Stockholm. The Farnese Palace, one of the greatest houses in the city, became her home and one of the most important centres of Roman intellectual life. Her social life bloomed and she became friendly with most of the great families of Rome, often staging plays and concerts for them at the Farnese. Some refused her invitations, embarrassed by her strange masculine dress, bold manners and brazen almost vulgar wit. Their misgivings increased when it became known that she had ordered the fig leaves be removed from all the male statues in the palace.

All that was missing for Christina was the emotional intimacy that Ebba Sparre had provided and she wrote to her claiming that in Rome 'I have seen no woman who can compete with you for loveliness ... I belong to you so utterly that it would be impossible for you ever to lose me until the day I die.' Yet, rumours persisted in Rome that Christina had enjoyed male lovers too, including the Marchese Monaldeschi, who attempted to betray her and was murdered by her guards. The scandal occurred in 1657, when Christina had visited the French court at Fontainebleau and caused considerable embarrassment to her host Louis XIV (1638–1715; King of France 1643–1715). She shocked the ladies of the French court with her masculine appearance and demeanour but most of all by the boldness of her conversation. When visiting the ballet with Christina, the Duchess of Monpensier recalled that:

she surprised me very much, applauding the parts which pleased her, taking God to witness, throwing herself back in her chair, crossing her legs, resting them on the arms of her chair, and assuming other postures, such as I had never seen taken ... She was in all respects a most extraordinary creature.

Yet, there was evidence of a more credible relationship between Christina and Cardinal Decio Azzolino (1623–89), a high official at the Vatican who was known to have had several previous lovers. As Azzolino became a frequent visitor to the Farnese Palace, Christina underwent another startling conversion, this time in her dress. Perhaps in response to Azzolino's attentions, she began appearing in feminine jewellery and gowns with revealing necklines. Inevitably the rumours grew and it was claimed that she had secretly had a child by Azzolino.

In a revealing insight into her complex sexuality, she told a friend at this time that she was relieved to have been born a woman after all, for if a man she would certainly have lived a life of total debauchery. But this appears to be defensive boasting rather than a true confession of sublimated desires. The truth was that whenever the opportunity of intimacy occurred in her life, she had always shied away from physical contact. Even the great love she undoubtedly bore for Ebba Sparre may well have stopped short of physical sex.

When Charles Gustav died in 1660, Christina returned briefly to Sweden but the lure of Rome proved too powerful and she soon returned to the city that had given her refuge. Her eccentric behaviour now began to irritate her benefactor, the Pope, at a time when her income from Sweden could no longer match her extravagance. In 1668, as her financial affairs became increasingly chaotic, she made a valiant attempt to economize by moving from the Farnese to a more modest residence at the Palazzo Riario.

When she died in 1689 the Pope, against her express wishes, had Christina's body embalmed and brought to St Peter's in Rome, where she was buried under the high altar. An isolated and enigmatic figure to the end, Christina of Sweden is perhaps fittingly the only woman ever to be buried in the crypt of St Peter's Basilica.

ENGLAND AND THE QUADRUPLE ALLIANCE

A curious fact of history is that while homosexuals were widely persecuted throughout Europe during the Middle Ages, England appears to have been free of homophobia and was spared the murderous zeal of the Holy Inquisition. Although Henry VIII's Buggery Act of 1533 prescribed the death penalty for sodomy in England, there is no record of any trials for the practice throughout the entire Tudor period. Sexual offences appear to have been seen more as spiritual than temporal crimes: Mary I (1516–1558; Queen of England 1553–58) repealed the act in 1553, whereas Elizabeth I restored it as a felony six years later. In 1607, however, sodomy was proposed as a far more serious offence by the leading English jurist Sir Edward Coke, in his *Laws of England*. Although a liberal interpreter of most laws, Coke was particularly disapproving of sodomy. He saw it as a crime as serious as treason itself. In Coke's view murder, rape, arson and burglary were far less heinous than the dreaded offence of sodomy.

Three years after Coke had completed *Laws*, one of the most notorious cases of homosexuality ever brought to court in England focused attention on the crime. In 1631, Mervyn Touchet, Earl of Castlehaven, along with two of his servants were accused of sodomy and also of the rape of Lady Castlehaven. Their trial was conducted before the House of Lords and a succession of witnesses described in lurid detail how Castlehaven and his men had indulged in mutual masturbation and mock intercourse, although no penetration had taken place. In a radical departure from legal precedents, the House of Lords upheld that charges of sodomy could be justly applied even if penetration had not occurred. The shadow of Sir Edward Coke's opinion hung ominously over the trial and

Castlehaven and his men were swiftly convicted and executed. With time this harsh interpretation was seen to be so unjust that later judges ignored the precedent and only imposed the death penalty if anal intercourse had occurred. This became written law in 1781 and men accused of sodomy could only be executed if both anal penetration and internal emission of semen were proven.

Seldom were English aristocrats charged with offences other than treason and none before Lord Castlehaven had been associated with a crime of a sexual nature. The English had been appalled to discover that sodomy was not just a sin practised by immoral French and Italians. Yet the mockery that greeted the bisexual William III (1650–1702; King of England, Scotland and Ireland 1689–1702) and his two Dutch male favourites, William Bentinck and Arnold Keppel, when they arrived in England, in 1688, was less motivated by contempt for their homosexuality than by political hostility and disdain for all foreigners. A people that had earlier witnessed James I fawning over his favourites, Robert Carr and George Villiers, was not easily shocked by the dour Dutchman and his boyfriends.

This characteristically English disregard of others' foibles persisted into the early 18th century and contrasted dramatically with the violent homophobia that later exploded in the supposedly more liberal Dutch Republic. There, 57 men were executed for sodomy in one year alone and almost 200 more were forced into exile because of accusations of homosexuality. The witch-hunt began in 1730 when a soldier named Zacharias Wilsma was arrested for sodomy. His testimony revealed that homosexual groups existed in most of the towns throughout Holland. The mania that gripped the country was almost as hysterical as the 'tulip-mania' of a century earlier, when the normally staid Dutch appeared to go crazy in gambling vast sums on the price of mere flower bulbs. The nationwide search for sodomites led to 250 arrests with a further 100 men managing to evade capture and flee into exile.

Why this sudden attack on supposed sexual deviants occurred after decades of social tolerance can perhaps be explained by changes in the country's social and economic circumstances. After a century of hard won independence and economic prosperity, Holland was faced with new, unexpected challenges. Commercial prosperity, for which the Dutch were famous, had abruptly declined when Britain began vying for the supremacy of the seas and world trade. As a result, unemployment spread throughout the country. At the same time disillusionment with religion led to church attendances falling and inns and taverns doing a brisk trade. Dutch Protestant culture also appeared to be losing ground to the Catholic influenced arts and customs of France and Italy, where it was assumed that homosexuality flourished. Evidence of this corruption could clearly be seen on the streets, where men had abandoned traditional sober colours in favour of effeminate French-derived flamboyance. The suspicion grew that this sartorial display was some sort of Catholic plot and that young sodomites were seeking to recruit others to their decadent cause.

In the same way that witches had traditionally been blamed for harvest failures, still born children or other local catastrophes, so were the homosexuals in Dutch society blamed for these otherwise inexplicable national disasters. The Dutch government introduced a bill that made sodomy a felony and began offering rewards to anyone with information on local sodomites. Predictably hundreds came forward, eager to settle a dispute with a neighbour or out of envy for someone more prosperous than themselves. Those so denounced were swiftly brought to trial and, when found guilty, executed. As with the Salem witch trials in Massachusetts in 1692, the rural community was as involved as the town dwellers thus challenging the popular belief that such so-called acts of depravity were confined to the urban elite. In 1731, 24 men and boys were strangled and then burned in the village of Faan, although it was later revealed that the magistrate concerned had used the charges of sodomy to settle a personal score and eliminate his political opponents. The Dutch press took up the anti-sodomy cause and a torrent of virulently anti-homosexual pamphlets, broadsheets, verse and moralistic tracts appeared, with some of it being published abroad in Britain.

Suspicion that Britain was also facing a similar moral decline at the hands of the dreaded sodomite had begun a few years earlier

43

when the first of the 'Molly houses' was discovered in London. Feminine mannerisms, cross-dressing and the use of female names by some men had become noticeable on the streets of London, where many single young men had migrated in search of work due to industrialization. Their meeting places were taverns and private houses that became known as Molly houses after the old name for a female prostitute. By the mid-1720s, over 20 such establishments were located throughout the city. The best known was an establishment run by Margaret Clap (Mother Clap) in Field Lane, Holborn, which was raided in 1726 by the Bow Street Runners, the only effective police in London at the time. The decision had been at the instigation of the Society for the Reformation of Manners (founded in 1691), a crusading organization that had used its members as agents provocateurs in the Molly houses. As the unfortunate men, many still in drag, were carted off to Bow Street they were attacked by a crowd of whores who were convinced that they were losing trade to these imposters. Three of those arrested at Mother Clap's were hanged for sodomy in May 1726 and the rest were either fined or thrown into prison. Clap herself got a two-year sentence for encouraging the vice. What emerged during the trial was that these meeting places, like the Cleveland Street establishment that would lead to the downfall of Oscar Wilde almost 200 years later, provided a unique meeting place for every social class in England – from aristocrats to street boys.

The shocking news that such places even existed – virtual brothels for the use of gay men – provoked a scandal and a witch-hunt similar to the one that would take place in Holland a few years later. Among those attacked were two inoffensive clergymen, the Reverend John Fenwick and the Reverend V. P. Littlehales, who were both suspected of being homosexual. As the mob approached their homes, they fled for their lives to exile in France. Their flight was taken as a sign of guilt and gave credence to the suspicion that sodomy was being encouraged by the Church of England. Publications appeared in both England and Holland, detailing the horrors of sodomy. None was more doom-laden and fatuous than the anonymous *The Reasons for the Growth of Sodomy in England* written in 1729. This warned of the dangers awaiting wealthy young Englishmen when they made their Italian Grand Tour. Drawn to such dens of iniquity as Florence, where Gian Gastone de Medici (1671–1737) was known to be a notorious sodomite, England's finest were in grave danger of seduction. The author of the pamphlet even attributed the popularity of opera and pantomime in London to this perfidious Italian corruption. Another sign of the contamination were the English houses being built in the Palladian style by young aristocrats returning from Italy. The pamphlet expressed the widespread belief that aestheticism encouraged sodomy, was incompatible with traditional British character and that a man should be hunting or shooting in the open air rather than contemplating paintings or gazing at classical statues of male nudes.

Another moralist, Bishop Joseph Hall (1574–1656), warned innocent young Englishmen that in travelling south to Italy, and to Venice in particular, they were entering 'the jawes of danger'. This sentiment was wholeheartedly endorsed by Dr Johnson's friend, Mrs Thrale, who thought of Italy that 'whoever lives long in it must be contaminated ... no other country has been so long and consistently associated with erotic freedom'. This was the generally accepted view of many Englishmen – that the dark legacy of the orgiastic Roman emperors still prevailed and that, as the author Daniel Defoe (1660–1731) put it in verse, 'Lust chose the Torrid Zone of Italy / Where blood ferments in Rapes and Sodomy.' Such dangers might well have surreptitiously appealed to the poet Thomas Gray (1716–71) and his friends Horace Walpole (1717–97), Richard West (d.1742), and Thomas Ashton, who set off on their own Grand Tour to Italy in March 1739.

The melancholic Gray, the son of a lazy, selfish, abusive and alcoholic businessman, was the only survivor of 12 children. After a miserable early childhood he went to Eton College in 1725, where he found happiness in the friendship of other boys. Like Lord Byron at Harrow, these relationships became passionate affairs and, again like Byron, Gray read enthusiastically about Greek Love. His closest friends at Eton and later at Cambridge were Horace Walpole, son of Prime Minister Sir Robert Walpole (1676–1745) and the most formidable aesthete of his day, Richard West, son of Ireland's Lord Chancellor and Thomas Ashton. Together they formed what they grandly called the Quadruple Alliance, in which they shared a common interest in music, literature and art. Walpole's vivacious character, in particular, captivated the reticent Gray who became infatuated with the considerably wealthier young aristocrat. Like Gray, Walpole would never marry and he confined his heterosexual relationships to a succession of unconsummated flirtations with unmarriageable women, some of whom, such as Anne Seymour Damer (1748–1828) and Mary Berry (1763–1852), were said by their contemporaries to be lesbian.

Having come of age, Thomas Gray inherited a modest legacy that gave him the financial independence needed to broaden his artistic horizons. He celebrated modestly by taking up the harpsichord and agreeing to join his fellow members of the Quadruple Alliance on a Grand Tour to Italy. Walpole, always guarded throughout his life about his sexuality, was clearly emotionally drawn to Gray. A recent biographer, Timothy Mowl, has claimed that Walpole had fallen in love with Henry Fiennes-Clinton, the 9th Earl of Lincoln (1720–94), while at Eton and had enjoyed a sexual affair with him at Cambridge, and would renew the affair when they met later in Italy so provoking Gray's jealousy. None of this friction was apparent when they set off in the spring of 1738 on their Grand Tour, with Walpole and Gray travelling together as a couple and the wealthy Walpole paying the expenses for them both. In Paris they exchanged their staid English dress for the latest French dandified fashions. At the end of the first year they crossed the Alps and entered Italy, visiting all the great cities from Venice to Naples as they progressed south. Walpole's political connections meant that they were welcomed everywhere by the leading British diplomats in Italy. Inevitably, the constant proximity with each other began to sour the relationship between the volatile and gregarious Walpole and the solitary and studious Gray. At Reggio the tension exploded into a violent quarrel exacerbated by Gray's jealousy of the Earl of Lincoln. It resulted in an ill-tempered parting, with Gray leaving alone for Venice.

In 1742 Gray returned to Peterhouse College, Cambridge, to study law but was soon diverted by the more agreeable contemplation of ancient Greek literature. There Gray's affections for his friend Richard West were rekindled at a time when West was increasingly troubled by family problems and his own declining health. The fast-declining West replaced Walpole as Gray's emotional confidant and inspired Gray's first major poem 'Ode on the Spring'. Gray sent it to West on the very day that his friend died at the age of 26. This tragic event had a profound effect on the acutely sensitive Gray and his grief became the spur for an unprecedented outburst of creative activity. Within a few months be had completed his 'Sonnet on the Death of Mr West', 'Ode to Adversity' and his second most famous poem 'Ode on a Distant Prospect of Eton College'. Then still moved by contemplations of West's death and inspired by the tranquil setting of the parish church at Stoke Poges, Gray began composing his 'Elegy Written in a Country Churchyard'.

Gray was to remain in Cambridge for the rest of his life and became the most reclusive academic in the university. Shunning the social pleasures of college life, he devoted himself to contemplation and study. His attraction to other men remained, however, and he was drawn to Norton Nicholls, a young undergraduate at Trinity Hall. As discreet as he was reclusive, Gray made sure that his homosexual feelings were only expressed in his verse. The persecutions in Holland and the scandal of the Molly houses made him profoundly cautious of openly betraying his emotions. He was also aware of the fate of a fellow lecturer who had let his emotions get the better of him.

In the year that Gray had set out on his Grand Tour, the Reverend Robert Thistlethwaite, Warden of Wadham College, Oxford, was tried in College for sexually assaulting a student, William French. The student's tutor, John Swinton, was also accused of homosexual practices. Found guilty, Thistlethwaite jumped bail and escaped to exile in France. Obscene verses appeared mocking Thistlethwaite, the most celebrated being the following limerick: 'There once was a Warden of Wadham / Who approved of the folkways of Sodom / For a man might, he said, Have a very poor head / But be a fine Fellow, at bottom.' Such scurrilous verse would have horrified the fastidious Gray, making him even more determined not to let his attraction take any physical form. As the biographer Robert Gleckner has written 'he knew the existence of temptations which could not for one moment be contemplated by one who had been all his life long, a strict observer of the laws of God and the laws of men.'

Then, in 1769, after decades of suppressing his emotions, the 53-year-old Gray fell completely and openly in love with a Swiss student named Charles Victor de Bonstetten. Captivated by the young man's beauty and enthusiasm for his poetry, Gray became utterly devoted to him, telling a friend that 'I never saw such a boy, our breed is not made on this model'. This sudden erotic friendship in his later years may well have been the most profound emotional experience of Gray's life. When de Bonstetten left Cambridge the following year to return to Switzerland, Gray was grief-stricken. His subsequent letters to him after his departure reveal just how intensely he felt their separation. Gray's health had never been robust and, while he was making plans to visit Switzerland, he fell seriously ill. Gray died in his rooms at Pembroke College on 30 July 1771 and was laid to rest in the same churchyard vault at Stoke Poges that he had immortalized.

While Gray had taken refuge in study and a life of quiet contemplation to sublimate the emotional desires for other men, his old friend Horace Walpole resolved similar temptations by leading a life of unceasing activity in composing thousand of letters to friends and acquaintances. Only once did Walpole come out and declare his passion for another man, his cousin, Henry Seymour Conway, who brusquely rejected the approach as being 'notoriously impious and contrary to nature'. Walpole never ventured to reveal his true feelings again, maintaining a nostalgic longing for what might have been and fondly recalling the pleasure and freedom he had enjoyed with Gray and the other members of the Quadruple Alliance in Florence. In spite of his many achievements, Walpole's was a life full of regret and he once sadly told a friend he had 'a million times repented returning to England where I was never happy, nor expect to be'.

THE SCANDAL OF WILLIAM BECKFORD

Not all homosexuals fascinated by classical art in the 18th century were as inhibited as Horace Walpole and Thomas Gray. Bolder spirits, such as the German Johann Winckelmann (1717–68), were at the forefront of European scholarship but made little attempt to disguise their sexual predilections.

The son of a poor shoemaker, Winckelmann escaped from poverty through his own determination and brilliant intellect. In 1748, he discovered the beauties of ancient Greek art while serving as librarian to Count Heinrich von Bünau (1697–1762) at Nothnitz, near Dresden. This inspired his *Reflections on the Painting and Sculpture of the Greeks*, a work that led to Winckelmann being acknowledged as the greatest classical art historian of his day. Winckelmann stated his firm conviction that 'those who are observant of beauty only in women, and are moved little or not at all by the beauty of men, seldom have an impartial, vital, inborn instinct for beauty in art'. As controversial in his actions as he was contentious in his opinions, his decision in 1754 to convert to Roman Catholicism – just as Christina of Sweden had previously done – shocked his Lutheran friends far more than the growing rumours of his homosexuality.

For this reason and because of Rome's well-established reputation for sexual, if not religious, tolerance he decided to take up residence there. Living in self-imposed exile in the city Winckelmann would not be subject to the same public condemnation of homosexuals that would later drive his near contemporary, William Beckford (1760–1844), into a more unwilling exile from England. In Rome, Winckelmann was able to behave in a relatively open manner – pursuing relationships with younger men without hindrance. When

49

caught *in flagrante delicto* with a young man by the heterosexual adventurer Giacomo Casanova, Winckelmann came up with an ingenious explanation. With total aplomb he asked Casanova not to be surprised by what he had just seen as his studies had led him to admire the ancients 'who, as you know, were all buggers without concealing it ... I decided to illuminate myself by practise, hoping that by analysing the matter my mind would acquire the light necessary for distinguishing between true and false'. This brazen attitude to life and the compulsion to take chances would eventually lead to Winckelmann's premature death. While in Trieste, in June 1768, awaiting a ship to take him back to Rome, the historian picked up a young man named Francesco Arcangeli and after taking him to his hotel showed him the gold and silver medals he had been awarded. The following day Arcangeli returned with a knife and repeatedly stabbed Winckelmann in a frenzied sexual attack. Arcangeli then fled, leaving Winckelmann to die in agony.

Before meeting his nemesis in the form of this violent young Italian, Johann Winckelmann had been recognized as the one person that all English aesthetes on the Grand Tour sought out in Rome. Among them was William Beckford, whose lack of sexual discretion would bring about his own spectacular downfall in English society.

Beckford was considered one of the most eligible young men in 18th-century England. He was the wealthiest commoner in the land with a family fortune derived from sugar plantations on the island of Jamaica. The Beckford fortune had been established by William's grandfather, who used his governorship of the island to fill his own coffers. When his own father died in 1770, William inherited, at the age of 10, an annual income of £70,000 from Jamaica and a lump sum of £1.5m together with the huge Palladian pile of Fonthill Splendens in Wiltshire. Interestingly, the Beckford estate had once belonged to Mervyn Touchet, Earl of Castlehaven, who had been executed for homosexual crimes more than a century earlier.

Beckford's father had been an unsophisticated, almost brutish man known to his Parliamentary colleagues as 'The Alderman'. His son could not have been more different; thin and delicate but possessed of great intelligence and an incredibly fertile imagination combined with deep aesthetic sensibilities. The family mansion that William inherited was surprisingly, given the Alderman's coarse character – so full of such wild rococo extravagance that it had a profound effect on the child's imagination.

William Beckford's taste for the exotic was further encouraged by his drawing master, the Russian-born painter Alexander Cozens (1717–86), who told him of the wonders of St Petersburg and encouraged him to read the tales of *The Arabian Nights*. Cozens also introduced the precocious boy to magic and occultism, which led him at 17 to write *The Vision*, a surreal tale set in some imagined eastern land. Two years later, and long before Wordsworth and Coleridge popularized the romance of the area, Beckford travelled in the Lake District, and wrote emotionally of the sublime grandeur of the landscape. The wonders of nature also encouraged his love of animals and his contempt for the blood sports so beloved of his fellow English country gentlemen. He later recalled meeting many such gentlemen when he first journeyed abroad to Geneva writing that they 'only smell of the stable, eat roast beef, drink, speak bad French, go to Lyons and come back with manly disorders'.

After 18 months in Geneva the 17-year-old Beckford had his first homosexual experience with a young man of his own age, whose dark eyes, Beckford wrote, 'drank eager draughts of pleasure from my sight, whose inmost soul was dissolved in tenderness when by chance he touched me'. When news of this romantic encounter reached England (Beckford had been particularly indiscreet in his letters), his horrified mother boarded the next boat to France en route to Geneva to bring back her foolish son before the relationship could be consummated. Beckford's character as a romantic sybarite was now firmly set and he wrote in his journal: 'I am determined to enjoy my dreams, my phantasies and all my singularity however irksome and discordant to the wordlings round me. In spite of them, I will be happy'. In the light of what was to follow for Beckford these would be sad and ironic words.

Two years earlier, while on a tour of English country houses in 1779, Beckford had met and fallen in love with an 11-year-old boy who would prove to be the cause of his disgrace and long exile from England. This was the exceptionally pretty William 'Kitty' Courtney (1768–1835), the son and heir to the Earl of Devon and Beckford's own nephew. In the boy's childishness, Beckford saw the reflection of his own fast-vanishing innocence. He made him the object of a long and passionate correspondence. Beckford made little attempt to disguise his feelings for 'Kitty' in either the Beckford or the Courtney households. Appalled at the prospect of the inevitable disaster, Beckford's tutor, Mr Lettice, attempted to distract him by suggesting another trip to the Lakes. However, on his return to Fonthill, Beckford continued his pursuit of the underage boy. Matters were complicated by the fact that Beckford had begun an affair with Louisa, the wife of his second cousin Peter Beckford. His letters to her contain similar breathless confessions of his all-embracing passion: 'I am cast into prophetic Trances. Lost in Dreams and majic (sic) slumbers my Hours glide swiftly away.' By now Beckford's mother was aware of these dangerous passions and persuaded her son to embark on a Grand Tour proper with Lettice.

Predictably, the romantic Beckford fell completely in love with Italy and with Venice, in particular. There, he met two sisters and a brother. When one of the girls complained that she had fallen in love with him but that he cruelly did not return her feelings, Beckford coolly replied that it was not the girls who attracted him but their handsome brother. Unable to comprehend such a statement, she attempted a dramatic if half-hearted attempt at suicide by poisoning. His highly embarrassed hosts sent him off on a prolonged sightseeing tour but Beckford could not avoid controversy for long.

In Lucca Beckford became so fascinated by the castrato singer Pacchierotti that he adopted a similar falsetto singing tone himself. Moving on to Naples he assumed the role of confidante to Catherine, the first wife of Sir William Hamilton, the great art collector, who became his mentor. Realizing that Beckford stood at the crossroads of his own sexuality, Catherine advised him to abandon his passion for young men as 'infamy, eternal infamy (my soul freezes while I write the word) attends the giving way to the soft alluring of a criminal passion'. Even when he had returned to England, Catherine wrote constantly urging him to be on his guard.

Whatever the moral and sexual dilemmas William Beckford struggled with, he still appeared to English society as one of the most eligible men in the country with a vast fortune to enjoy. He moved in London society, met the Prince of Wales and had his portrait painted by Sir Joshua Reynolds and George Romney. His self-indulgence became legendary with the celebrations for his 21st birthday in 1781, which lasted three days and included dramatic firework displays, bonfires and performances by three leading Italian opera stars of the day. At Christmas, a few months later, Beckford gave an even more extravagant party organized by Philippe Jacques de Loutherbourg, a master of special effects, and which lasted several nights. News that one room at Fonthill had been decorated as a 'Demon Temple' led to gossip in nearby Bath that black magic and satanic orgies had taken place.

Still, his obsession with 'Kitty' Courtney, now at Westminster School, continued unabated and in December 1787 it appeared to have found physical fulfilment as revealed in a letter that Beckford wrote to 'Kitty' expressing his delight 'at last night's events ... [when he had] enjoyed the prize and revelled till ten in the morning'.

Shortly afterwards another event occurred that would indirectly lead to Beckford's social downfall and exile. William Courtney's mother died and his aunt Catherine, who had been rejected by William Beckford, replaced her as guardian of the boy. Catherine's husband was Lord Loughborough, a no-nonsense Scottish lawyer who championed the burning of women for coining (tampering with the coinage for gain) and clearly despised the self-indulgent world that William Beckford represented. Under pressure from his mother, Beckford agreed to buy a set seat in Parliament and to marry Lady Margaret Gordon, who was described by the jealous Louisa Beckford as 'a cold-blooded disciple of pale-eyed chastity'.

Expecting little from the union, Beckford set off to spend the next year in Europe with his new bride. Although he did not love

Lady Margaret, Beckford soon found himself growing fond of his new bride and the sweet simplicity of her character. Even his obsession with William Courtney appeared to be fading as he found himself becoming ever closer to his modest new companion 'who loves everything that amuses me'.

When the Beckfords returned to England in 1784, 'Kitty' had transformed from a pretty young boy into an effeminate youth 'interested only in millinery'. Redemption could only come, Beckford decided, if 'Kitty' was sent to be tutored by his friend, the Reverend Samuel Henley and he implored Courtney's father to agree. But while the Beckfords had been abroad, Lord Loughborough had been strengthening his position in the family. Apart from loathing Beckford personally he also bore a deep resentment against his political mentor, Lord Thurlow.

Loughborough now made his move, warning Lord Courtney to be wary of Beckford. When Beckford foolishly agreed to visit the Courtneys at Powderham Castle for a month, Loughborough laid a trap for Beckford with 'Kitty' as the bait. On their departure Loughborough claimed to have found Beckford in Kitty's bedroom in compromising circumstances. Loughborough had discovered some of Beckford's most passionate letters to the boy and he revealed the contents of these to Lady Margaret's brother Lord Strathavon, who rushed to Fonthill, ordered his sister to leave with him and when she refused slapped Beckford's face challenging him to a duel which he, in turn, refused. This was a real crisis as the means for William Beckford's ruin lay firmly in the hands of his enemy Loughborough. At worst Loughborough, as one of the most senior law officers in the country, could insist that Beckford be charged with sodomy, still a capital offence. Even if not executed, Beckford could face the ignominy and the brutality of being placed in the pillory.

Beckford's only hope was that the crime would be difficult to prove although the incriminating letters now in Loughborough's possession were powerful circumstantial evidence. Loughborough's motive in persecuting his victim has been attributed by Beckford's biographer, Brian Fothergill, as jealousy. While Loughborough had been forced to claw his way up in society by hard work, Beckford had been handed immense wealth and an indulgent lifestyle. At a hastily convened council-of-war with Lord Thurlow and John Lettice at Fonthill, it was decided that the only possible course of action was immediate flight before Loughborough could arrange Beckford's arrest. Beckford had to leave England at once and stay abroad until the storm abated.

William Beckford set off to Dover alone – after two previous miscarriages Margaret was again pregnant and unable to endure the rigors of the journey. When the seas at Dover were too rough to allow a ship to sail, Beckford realized that by leaving England like a fugitive he would only confirm his guilt. He decided to call Loughborough's bluff and return to Fonthill to face his accuser, confident that his wife would fully support him.

As the weeks passed it seemed that Beckford might have made the best decision, for Loughborough was well aware that he had insufficient evidence to make a case. Instead, he decided to destroy Beckford's standing in society by showing him to be little more than an extremely wealthy pervert. On 27 November 1784 he leaked the story to the *Morning Herald* newspaper and an article appeared showing mock concern over 'The rumour concerning a Grammatical mistake of Mr B – and the Hon Mr C – in regard to the genders' and going on to castigate 'characters who regardless of Divine, Natural and Human law, sink themselves below the lowest class of brutes in the most preposterous rites.' Other newspapers took up the scandal, sparking a media witch-hunt. Even the government was dragged into the scandal when, during a critical general election year, it was pointed out that it was about to create one of the two miscreants, William Beckford, a peer. When the story reached George III (1738–1820; King of Great Britain and Ireland 1760–1820), he issued an order to reject any application for a peerage for Beckford and told those around him that he personally thought the villain should hang.

As in any scandal the general public clamoured to know more of the salacious details and the press was happy to oblige. The English aristocracy appeared fascinated by the affair, with

Lord Pembroke writing from Italy to ask his son to find out more about 'the exact business, how, when, and by whom, and with whom discovered'.

In a clumsy attempt to exonerate her son, Beckford's mother issued a statement claiming that it was all a terrible mistake. Her son had really been conducting a clandestine relationship with a married woman and had been using William Courtney as a messenger boy to carry letters. Beckford became a figure of public mockery and his very name the butt of working men's humour all over Britain. Loughborough had succeeded beyond his wildest dreams in the social destruction of William Beckford – as Sir William Hamilton commented sadly 'the verdict of society has gone against him, and from that sentence there is no appeal'.

As would happen in the soured relationship between Oscar Wilde and Lord Alfred Douglas, Beckford began blaming the younger man for his betrayal. Courtney was damaged almost as much by the scandal as Beckford himself, however. Courtney seems to have been more actively and exclusively gay than his supposed seducer; he never married and often behaved indiscreetly. By 1811 an Essex magistrate had collected enough evidence to convict Courtney of unnatural crimes and on hearing that a warrant had been issued for his arrest, he fled to exile in France, where he lived in obscurity for the next 24 years.

For a man of Beckford's ebullient character, his self-imposed imprisonment at Fonthill was almost unbearable and made even more harrowing by the ill health of Lady Margaret. Smouldering resentment against the pious hypocrisy of English society finally goaded him into action and he declared that he would rather face the rotten eggs and fruit in a London pillory than remain in abject contrition at Fonthill, 'my mouth pursed up into a demure simper'.

He decided to leave England in June 1785 for Switzerland, where the Beckfords were welcomed at the town of Vevey by several old friends. Free at last of the constant attacks from newspapers, Beckford found peace again and began working quietly on his novel *Vathek*. Having unexpectedly found love with his wife, Beckford suffered another blow when Margaret died from puerperal fever in May 1786, 12 days after giving birth to a healthy daughter. She was just 24 years old and the loss left Beckford utterly bereft.

Beckford moved on to Lisbon, where he became close friends with the family of a local aristocrat, the Marquis de Marialvas. Captivated by Beckford's charm, the Marquis encouraged him to consider an engagement to his daughter, but it was, in reality, her 13-year-old brother, Don Pedro, that had caught Beckford's eye. Beckford's diary entries clearly reveal that the boy was his new obsession: 'He loves me, I have tasted the sweetness of his lips; his dear eyes have confessed the secret of his bosom', he wrote. However, Beckford appeared determined not to repeat the disaster of the Courtney relationship. Instead, he diverted his amorous attentions to Gregorio Franchi (1770–1828), a young musician of an Italian family living in Lisbon, who would later join him in England. When he left for Spain after 10 months in Lisbon, Beckford was much restored in spirits and ready to come to terms with his past.

Life in Madrid proved equally gratifying, with Beckford indulging his bisexual preferences with the 18-year old married daughter of the Duchesse de la Vauguyon and her younger brother 'a smart stripling with wild hair and a low Grecian forehead'.

Joined by Gregorio Franchi, Beckford moved on to Paris, where he witnessed the early days of the French Revolution (1787–99). What was happening in France would not only change the course of European history, but would also dramatically alter the status of homosexuals in French society. First the National Convention abolished the laws governing consensual sodomy and when Bonaparte became Consul, the *Code Napoleon* affirmed the principle that a citizen's sexuality was not the business of the state. This attitude was to prevail for over a century and France became the only European nation not to differentiate legally between hetero- and homosexuality until the Vichy government brought in homophobic laws during the Second World War (1939–45). Appropriately, Napoleon's enlightened reform was introduced into the Convention and monitored by his Consul, the overtly gay Jean Jacques Cambacérès. While this change in legal status did not really affect William Beckford, it must have given him satisfaction to be present at a time when the first truly modern approach to homosexuality was shown. However, Beckford seemed unaware of the tumultuous times he was experiencing and continued living a grand lifestyle with never less than 30 horses in the cavalcade whenever he went out. He seems to have paid little attention to this inappropriate display of wealth at a time when the French Committee of Public Safety were stamping out such aristocratic behaviour. Then, just as the French authorities began to take in interest in this spendthrift foreigner, the government of William Pitt (1759–1806; Prime Minister 1783–1801 and 1804–06) in London brought in an act declaring that any British citizen continuing to live in enemy France would be considered a traitor. Faced with total exclusion from England, Beckford decided, in March 1793, that he had little option other than to return and face British public opinion and Lord Loughborough's malevolence.

Beckford had long ago conceived the idea of building a high, 12.8 km (8 mile) long stone wall around the Fonthill demesne. Its purpose he claimed was to stop local hunts careering across his land, although symbolically it cut him off from the hostile outside world. Its construction began, together with that of a vast mansion with an astonishing tower over 91 metres (300 feet) high. This would be Beckford's architectural act of defiance, his personal ivory tower, defended by the great walls of Fonthill. Beckford next turned his attention to his own social and political rehabilitation. Having just returned from France, he proposed that he should be appointed a special envoy between the French and British governments to negotiate an agreement between the two nations. Unsurprisingly Pitt dismissed the offer, spurring the furious Beckford to compose a long and bitter personal attack on the Prime Minister in verse.

Finally realizing that there would be no future for him in public life, Beckford returned to Fonthill, where, with his capable but occasionally reckless architect James Wyatt (1746–1813), he threw himself into rebuilding the house. Beckford remained a social pariah and even when national hero Lord Nelson (1758–1805) dined at Fonthill in December 1800, accompanied by Sir William Hamilton (1730–1803) and his new wife, Emma (1761–1815), none of the local gentry were present. Those artists and composers who did attend were impressed by the burgeoning Gothic splendour of Fonthill Abbey and compared it favourably to Horace Walpole's seminal building at Strawberry Hill in Twickenham.

In 1806 both William Pitt and Loughborough died, removing at a stroke Beckford's two most dangerous enemies. That same year he resumed a closer contact with his daughter from his marriage with Margaret. His reputation made even this a controversial business and Beckford agreed at the family's request that she should not live with him at Fonthill. He had abandoned his bisexuality in favour of an exclusively homosexual relationship with Gregorio Franchi, who had followed Beckford to England and come to live with him at Fonthill. His bizarre taste persisted, however, and he imported a dwarf to be his doorkeeper and employed a harem of boy-servants, each of which was given an effeminate name such as 'Poupee', 'Mademoiselle Bion', 'Miss Butterfly', 'Countess Pox' and disapprovingly 'Mr Prudent Well-Sealed-up.' Apart from the servants there was a series of passions for various young male actors but Beckford appears to have shunned physical contact. Beckford also collected newspaper cuttings about homosexual scandals until the year of his death. Among them was an account of the arrest, trial and execution of the Vere Street group, published in the *Morning Chronicle* of 10 July 1810. His comments on the event are typical of his unique combination of sympathy and cynicism:

Poor sods – what a fine ordeal, what a procession, what a pilgrimage, what a song and dance, what a rosary [i.e., string of prisoners]! What a pity not to have a balcony in Bow Street to see them pass, and worse still not to have a magic wand to transform into a triumph the sorry sequence of events.

By the 1820s, even William Beckford's great wealth was exhausted and he was forced to sell Fonthill in 1823. He bought a smaller estate near Bath, where he built the Lansdowne Baghdad, a house with a much shorter tower than Fonthill. Now in his late 60s, he became respectably eccentric rather than scandalous, and was tolerated by society rather than accepted. In the opinion of one modern biographer, Alistair Sutherland, Beckford was 'as much a martyr as Wilde, and almost certainly a more interesting and civilized man'. He was immensely intelligent as well as a hedonist, a serious artist as well as a social rebel, and more honest than eccentric. One of his admirers was Lord Byron (1788–1824) who clearly realized the great similarity between the two. In 1809 they agreed to meet but at the last minute Beckford declined the offer saying that he found it too painful to be confronted by someone so very much like his younger self.

THE LADIES OF
LLANGOLLEN

Throughout the 18th century, public attention in England had largely been confined to male homosexuality and the supposed misdeeds of men, such as William Beckford. The idea that women could also indulge in same-sex activity was largely ignored or ridiculed. Without suitable physical equipment just how could penetration, the key legal requirement for a sodomy conviction, possibly take place?

In Europe the prospect of lesbianism was giving Catholic moralists far more concern after the rediscovery of the Greek poet Sappho's erotic verses during the Renaissance. In 1532 the Holy Roman Empire made sex between women an offence and in France two women were burned for cross-dressing and attempting to marry. The same fate later befell two Spanish nuns – which was seen as confirmation of the long-held popular belief that convents were a hotbed of unnatural vice. What brought new attention to the issue, later in that century, was the discovery by two Italian anatomists of the clitoris. Its relevance to sexual pleasure had been neglected by earlier generations of doctors. This posed a new threat to male dominance for it appeared that women could pleasure one other without the need of a man.

Further disquieting evidence of lesbianism occurred in 1721, when Catharina Linck (1687–1721) was sentenced to death in Germany. A persistent cross-dresser, she had served as a soldier in the Hanoverian, Prussian, Hessian and Polish armies and wisely revealed her true sex on only one occasion – when about to be shot by the enemy. Abandoning her military career, Linck 'married' a younger girl and settled down with her in the town of Halberstadt. There, she always dressed as a man and had 'intercourse' with her bride using a 'leather instrument'. When her mother-in-law discovered her true sex, Linck was arrested and convicted of 'abominable sodomy'. The jury had great difficulty in understanding just what female sodomy constituted, but nevertheless found the unfortunate woman guilty and she was beheaded.

To the English, cross-dressing and lesbianism were considered the vices of foreigners and had little to do with their own country. English women were deemed incapable of such behaviour, although the translator of *La Religieuse* (*The Nun*, written 1760, published 1796) by Denis Diderot (1713–84) explained his excision of one of the novel's more explicitly Sapphic scenes on the grounds that he was reluctant to shock his English readers. The French, however, 'are permitted a latitude which the English taste has forbidden'. This view of lesbianism as a foreign vice was even endorsed by law and, in a judgement as late as 1810, it was stated, without any contradiction, as being unknown in Britain.

What most concerned those who did believe that lesbianism existed was not the sexual act itself, but the serious deception of a woman posing as a man. English writer Henry Fielding (1707–54) used a case similar to that of the Linck affair as the basis for his novel *The Female Husband* (1746). It was based on the true story of Barbara Hill, a woman who had tried to enlist as a soldier before marrying Ann Steed in 1756, with whom she had already lived happily for five years. Hill was not punished on discovery but another woman, purporting to be a 'Samuel Bundy', was jailed in Southwark, London, soon after, for marrying a woman and defrauding her of her clothes and money. Such cases gave credence to rumours that women, particularly those in the aristocracy, were developing strong emotional relationships with each other, ones that might threaten male dominance in society. The satirical novel *The New Atlantis* (1709–10) by Mary de la Riviere Manley (1663–1724) fuelled this concern for it suggested the existence of a lesbian secret society known as the 'Bower of Bliss', whose members were a female Whig cabal bent on undermining male rule.

The historian Louis Crompton suggests that there were numerous cases of romantic relationships between aristocratic ladies at the time. Both daughters of James II (1633–1701; King of Great Britain 1685–88), Mary II (1662–94; wife of William III; Queen of England, Scotland and Ireland 1689–94) and Anne (1665–1714; Queen of Great Britain and Ireland 1702–14), were passionately attached to other women. Mary was constantly writing love letters to a beautiful younger woman, Frances Apsley (d.1727), in which she addressed her as 'husband' – for a long time these were thought to have been written to her husband, William III. Mary's sister Anne was equally obsessed by Frances and adopted the pen name 'Ziphares' from the 17th century drama of the time; Frances was 'Semandra'. Anne's principal love, however, was Sarah Churchill (1660–1744), the wife of the great military commander, John Churchill, the Duke of Marlborough. For two decades, Sarah was the Queen's most trusted confidante; the Queen abandoned formality when speaking to Sarah in private, addressing her always as 'Mrs Freeman' and was called 'Mrs Morley' in return. Eventually, Anne transferred her affections to a younger woman named Abigail Masham (d.1734). Angry and vengeful at being discarded, Sarah wrote Anne a letter in which she made a thinly veiled accusation of the Queen's lesbian activity with Masham, referring to a satirical verse of the time that contained the lines:

Her Secretary she was not
Because she could not write;
But had the Conduct and the Care
Of some dark Deeds at night.

What particularly alarmed politicians at this time was that through such intimate relationships well-placed women were beginning to have a profound influence on national policy, such as the appointment of ministers and military commanders – as Sarah's success in gaining command of the army for her husband, the Duke of Marlborough, had demonstrated.

The most celebrated example of female bonding in the late 18th century had no political implications, but radically altered the public perception of what a close female relationship could be. It began in 1778 when two Irish ladies from aristocratic families disguised themselves in men's clothing and ran away together. Instead of provoking scandal and criticism, their romantic escapade won the sympathy of the nation and they became known affectionately as the 'Ladies of Llangollen' after the Welsh village they chose to live in. The elder of the two, Lady Eleanor Butler (1739–1829), was a member of the once powerful family of Kilkenny that had governed Ireland under the Stuarts, but had later forfeited much of their land and wealth to the Crown. Sent to board at a convent in France, there Eleanor showed an aptitude for literature and languages, but on return to Ireland, and in spite of family pressure, she showed little interest in marriage. Her future partner was Sarah Ponsonby (1755–1831), a much younger girl, who lived just 12 miles from Kilkenny. She too came from an Anglo-Irish family, but had lost both her parents and her inheritance as a child. Virtually penniless, she had no option but to suffer the humiliation of joining her father's family at Woodstock. While attending a nearby boarding school in Kilkenny, the 13-year-old Sarah was visited by Eleanor Butler, 16 years her senior. The younger girl was fascinated by Eleanor's sophistication and knowledge of French culture, whereas Eleanor felt an instinctive need to protect the shy, younger girl.

The two women corresponded secretly for the next 10 years. Eleanor's mother, realizing that her 39-year-old daughter would never marry, urged her to enter a Catholic convent. Meanwhile, Sarah was being harassed by her guardian at Woodstock, Sir William Fownes. His wife, a distant relative of Sarah's, was in poor health and Fownes clearly saw his young ward as her future replacement. One evening in March 1778, Sarah could stand his sexual advances no longer. Dressed in men's clothing and armed with a pistol, she took her small dog and crept out of the house to where Eleanor Butler was waiting for her. They set off for the port of Waterford to sail to England, but after spending a night in a barn, the two women arrived at the dock to be confronted by angry members of both their families and were escorted back home. As no man had been involved, their conduct was declared 'void of serious impropriety'. However, they were determined to be together and a month later Eleanor made her way back to Woodstock. There, in front of her assembled relatives, Sarah Ponsonby announced that it was her firm intention 'to live and die with Miss Butler'. The following morning both women, accompanied by Sarah's maid, were gone. This time their escape was successful and they sailed to Milford Haven in Wales.

Their travels around England and Wales that summer were recorded in Sarah Ponsonby's journal, amusingly titled *Account of a Journey in Wales perform'd in May 1778 by Two Fugitive Ladies*. At end of their tour, they decided to settle together in a picturesque cottage in the Welsh hills, near Llangollen, which they renamed *Plas Newydd* or the 'New Place'.

As enthusiastic followers of the French philosopher Jean-Jacques Rousseau (1712–78), they decided to live by his principle that man should live in harmony with nature. Their problem in these early years was primarily financial for they had only small allowances provided by their families. When news of their romantic escapade reached London, it captured the imagination of their upper-class contemporaries. They were to become the most famous exponents of 'retirement' in England – a quest for rural idyll in which to contemplate nature and philosophy. It was a concept that was a natural progression from Rousseau's ideas and had already become popular with the upper classes throughout Europe. Even Marie Antoinette (1755–93; queen of France 1774–93) became a follower with her *Petit Hameau*, a mock farm in the grounds of Versailles, where she and her ladies dressed as milk maids, played with animals and milked the cows.

At Llangollen the ladies set about improving their land and their minds with the same energy that they had already devoted to studying languages, art and the sciences. Each year they enlarged and embellished their small cottage in the newly fashionable Gothic style, adding stained-glass windows and carved wood interiors. At a time when there were few decent hotels on the road to Holyhead, the Llangollen Ladies soon began attracting visitors. Their home became an essential stopping place for anyone of social or cultural standing travelling through the area. They were visited by all manner of distinguished people, including the poets Robert Southey (1774-1843), William Wordsworth (1770–1850), Percy Shelley (1792–1822) and Lord Byron, as well as Sir Walter Scott (1771–1832), Josiah Wedgwood (1730–1795) and George IV (1762–1830; king of united kingdom of Great Britain and Ireland 1820–30). Among their greatest admirers was the Duke of Wellington (1769–1852), to whom they gave a Spanish prayer book that he would later use during the Peninsular War (1808–14). Walter Scott's son-in-law, also a guest, commented tartly on their powdered hair, encountered more often in a man, and was staggered by their 'enormous' shoes and top hats worn in combination with female petticoats. Their eccentric dress appeared to produce gentle amusement rather than serious controversy. The actor Charles Matthews (1776–1835) described them as being like 'two dear old gentlemen' when seated at the dinner table wearing their dark cloth habits, well-starched cravats and black beaver hats. Matthews found it almost impossible to take his eyes off these 'dear antediluvian darlings' and dearly wished that he could pop Lady Eleanor 'under a bell jar and take her home to show his wife'.

Another of their guests, the German nobleman Prince Pückler-Muskau (1785–1871), found them charming hosts but at the same time slightly ridiculous. This was perhaps the secret of late Georgian society's undoubted fascination for the Llangollen Ladies. Unlike the forthright Christina of Sweden, striding through her courtiers dressed in male attire, these gentle ladies posed no threat. In their mountain retreat they were completely removed from either London or Dublin society and an aura of loving innocence characterized the impression they gave to their visitors. Nor was lesbianism much of a concern to an English society more fascinated by gossip of the male homosexual adventures of a William Beckford or a Lord Byron in foreign places. Even the moralistic Queen Charlotte (1744–1818), who had to contend with the sexual escapades of her own errant sons, became fascinated by their romantic exile and persuaded her husband, George III

(1738–1820; king of Great Britain and Ireland 1760–1820), to grant them a small pension of £200 a year.

Nonetheless, speculation about the exact nature of their relationship continued, provoked by their bold lifestyle. This was no backstairs affair but an unequivocal and open declaration of one woman's deepest commitment to another. Dr Johnson's friend, Hester Thrale (1740–1821), who became their neighbour in Wales, was at first wary of the ladies, believing that theirs was an immoral form of female friendship that had been imported from France, where Marie Antoinette was rumoured to preside over 'a set of monsters call'd by each other Sapphists.' As she got to know them better, however, Mrs Thrale was also won over and became their firm friend.

The writer Anne Lister, who wrote a remarkable and secret account of her life as a lesbian, was fascinated by the Ladies of Llangollen. As masculine in appearance as Eleanor Butler, Lister was equally committed to cross-dressing, but was acutely aware of the danger of her own sexuality. Perhaps Lister saw in their successful relationship a stark contrast to her own sad fate. She, too, had found the love of her life in a woman named Marianna Lawton, but Lawton had bowed to convention and made a loveless marriage of convenience. Anne's affair with Lawton continued for years after the marriage until Lawton, anxious to preserve her respectability and social position, abandoned her. Anne Lister's diaries were written in code and give an intimate account of her love for other women. After visiting the Ladies at Llangollen, Lister wrote, 'I cannot help thinking that surely it was not Platonic.' A century later, the great French novelist Colette (1873–1954), occasionally a cross-dresser herself, was equally captivated by this charming and enduring friendship, speculating about it in her study of homosexual relationships, *The Pure and the Impure*. Writing a century after Eleanor Butler's death, Colette imagines them being alive in the 1930s when they would 'own a car, wear dungarees, smoke cigarettes, have short hair and there would be a liquor bar in their apartment'. In fact, at the time of Colette writing this, Gertrude Stein (1874–1946) and Alice B. Toklas (1877–1967) were living out a similar sociable exile.

At a time when middle- and upper-class English women often entered loveless marriages solely to fulfil family and social obligations, such an intimate female friendship as undoubtedly existed between Eleanor Butler and Sarah Ponsonby was a bold and unusual statement. What the Ladies of Llangollen did so openly and so courageously was to set an example by defying both intense family pressure and social convention and living openly as a couple. They demonstrated their intimate relationship by signing their correspondence jointly and by mockingly naming one of their dogs 'Sappho'. Many were puzzled by the exact nature of their sexual arrangement, even such social conservatives as the Duke of Wellington preferred to believe that their relationship was purely platonic, and could only admire their pluck in settling in such wild and mountainous place. As the years passed, they were transformed by public approbation from local curiosities into national treasures. Some later feminists maintained that the Llangollen Ladies were motivated not by erotic passion but by a mutual desire to live as independent women without the control of men. This rather belittles the undoubted love that existed between them. In her journal Eleanor recalls one night of terrible headaches as Sarah lay beside her:

My kindest love did not sleep even for a moment the entire night but lay beside me watching and lamenting my illness and soothing by her tenderness the distressing pain in my head ... My beloved Sally never left me for a single moment.

Eleanor Butler died in June 1829, Sarah Ponsonby died two years later. They are buried together at St Collen Church in Llangollen. Two centuries after their death, their relationship remains an example of loving camaraderie between women and they have come to be regarded, in the words of biographer Elizabeth Mavor, as 'a paradigm of the heart's desire ... the perfect friends'.

LORD BYRON'S
PILGRIMAGE

When Lord Byron had written of his love for the choirboy John Eddleston, he compared it to the love of the Ladies of Llangollen. Byron boasted that he and Eddleston would outdo even those good ladies in their affection. Strangely, for such a volatile man of the world, Byron seems to have taken the quiet retiring pair as the model for a perfect romantic relationship, although the idea of Byron settling down with another man in some rural retreat is preposterous. Yet, their example continued to intrigue him and when he became a successful author he sent them a copy of his poem 'The Corsair' (published in 1814). Although Byron's heterosexuality had made him infamous throughout Europe as the archetypical male lover, it was his homosexuality that would lead to his social disgrace and exile from England. Until that moment and after the publication of his most successful poem 'Childe Harold' (Cantos I and II published in 1812, Cantos III and IV in 1818), he was the most sought after celebrity in London and he was welcomed in all the great Whig houses presided over by the Hollands, the Melbournes and the Jerseys. Every hostess in the city was eager to attract him and his appeal was made all the more irresistible because of his studied remoteness, his pale face and translucent skin that was compared to 'an alabaster vase lit up from within'. In March 1816, however, his rejected lover, Lady Caroline Lamb (1785–1828) – wife of British Prime Minister William Lamb (1779–1848) – revealed to Byron's wife Annabella (1792–1860) that he had confessed to her, not only his incestuous affair with his half-sister Augusta Leigh (1783–1851), but also his involvement in many homosexual relationships.

This act of revenge by Caroline Lamb would destroy the reputation of the most famous poet in England. As Byron later wrote 'my name has been completely blasted as if I were branded on my forehead'. Yet this was just one part of a bitter campaign that Caroline had planned. Increasingly unstable in her behaviour towards her husband William as well as to Byron, she had already attempted suicide in the poet's presence and behaved towards him with great malevolence. When she had written the words 'Remember me', by strange coincidence in Byron's copy of William Beckford's *Vathek*, the poet replied with the bitter lines:

> *Remember thee! Aye, doubt it not.*
> *Thy husband too shall think of thee!*
> *By neither shalt thou be forgot,*
> *Thou false to him, thou fiend to me!*

Although Lady Byron issued a statement dismissing the allegations against her husband as malicious gossip, she nevertheless signed a separation agreement the following month and four days later Byron drove to Dover and sailed from England never to return. Before he left, however, he unwisely ordered his publisher, John Murray, to print two angry satirical poems mocking his wife and her friend and self-appointed champion, Mary Anne Clermont. Although not openly published, the contents of the poems were leaked and attracted a vitriolic press campaign against Byron. At the instigation of the politician Henry Brougham (1778–1868), *The Champion* newspaper published the poems. This encouraged other assaults on Byron's character, most of them coming from a Tory press only too delighted to ridicule one of the most prominent critics of the Crown. The *Morning Chronicle* rushed into verse to wish good riddance to Byron:

> *His mad career of crimes and follies run*
> *And grey in vice, when life was scarce begun;*
> *He goes, in foreign lands prepared to find*
> *A life more suited to his guilty mind.*

Yet Byron also had his defenders in the press, not least the highly influential *Times* newspaper that hoped his self-imposed exile would be a short one. The radical journalist Leigh Hunt (1784–1859), a proven enemy of cant, lambasted in his own newspaper, *The Examiner*, these 'depraved speculations of the falsest and most brutal nature'. Nonetheless, the attacks had wounded Byron deeply and he deplored being compared to 'such worthies' of the ancient world as Nero, Apicius and Caligula, all of whom were either homo or bisexuals. The public, meanwhile, were happy to believe that this arrogant Lord, who had mocked so many British institutions, was capable of any kind of deviance. The Irish poet Tom Moore (1779–1852) watched the barrage of criticism unleashed on his friend with marked distaste, commenting that 'such an outcry was now raised against Lord Byron as, in no case of private life, perhaps, was ever before witnessed'.

At least one of the poet's friends, John Cam Hobhouse (1786–1869), thought that he should have brazened it out and not left England: 'There was not the slightest necessity even in appearance for his going abroad' he wrote. But after attending a party given by Lady Jersey, where he was snubbed by almost the entire company, Byron had come to accept his exile as inevitable. Nor was the contempt shown him confined to London high society, for Byron later claimed:

I was advised not to go to the theatres, lest I should be hissed, nor to my duty in parliament, lest I should be insulted by the way; even on the day of my departure my most intimate friend told me afterwards that he was under apprehension of violence from the people who might be assembled at the door of the carriage.

According to Hobhouse, Byron thought the tide of public opinion was so strong against him that he might even be assassinated. Byron's fears may well have been justified for it was an age when convicted or suspected homosexuals were liable to be attacked in the street. Much of this public aggression had been encouraged by the Society for the Suppression of Vice, an institution founded by William Wilberforce (1759–1833), who is better known for his involvement in the abolition of the British slave trade. From its establishment in 1802, the society's sanctimonious and self-imposed task was the encouragement of 'Piety and Virtue' and the prevention and punishment of 'Vice, Profaneness and Immorality'. Unfortunately, when the Byron scandal broke, the society was still basking in the success of its involvement in the Vere Street scandal, following the raiding of a London 'Molly house' in July 1810 when 27 men were arrested, two of whom were later hung at Newgate Prison.

Yet in the very year that Byron felt himself obliged to leave England, a significant step was taken to ameliorate the harsh treatment of homosexuals. The Member of Parliament Michael Angelo Taylor (1757–1834) sponsored a bill abolishing the use of the pillory for those convicted of sodomy. Although pillorying may appear a somewhat ludicrous punishment today, it was a form of public torture that could easily lead to death because the victims were often pelted with stones and bricks, as well as rubbish and dead cats. Moreover, the death penalty for sodomy was still in force and, in contrast to the rest of Europe, was now being rigorously imposed. Significantly, one of those who spoke on the bill, Sir Robert Heron, expressed the pious hope that if the pillory was abolished then the English upper classes should rigorously ostracize any of their number who dared commit the offence of sodomy. Taylor, a realist in such matters, replied that this was too much to expect as no powers or punishment could stop men committing 'this atrocious offence'. Yet there is no doubt that Byron's peers either spontaneously, or at Heron's behest, followed his advice to the letter by withdrawing their friendship and even their common civility from Lord Byron on the mere suspicion of his homosexuality.

A more detailed account of Byron's painful rejection was later given by Countess Teresa Guiccioli (1800–73), his last sustained heterosexual lover. In her *Recollections* she claims that he was 'cut' by his fellow peers in the House of Lords with only Lord Holland speaking to him, although 'others such as the Duke of Sussex, Lord Minto, Lord Lansdowne and Lord Grey would fain have acted in a like manner but they suffered themselves to be influenced by his enemies'.

Byron told her that it was not until he had crossed the Alps and joined her in Venice, that the sound of the baying mob finally left his ears. The pursuit of Byron bore an uncanny similarity to that of William Beckford 30 years earlier and that of Oscar Wilde 80 years later. Beckford had then complained to a friend that 'I have been hunted down and persecuted these many years. I have been stung and not allowed opportunities of changing the snarling, barking style you complain of ... No truce, no rebspite have I experienced since the first sporting licences were taken out.' Even Sir Walter Scott's positive review of Byron's 'Childe Harold' the following year served only to rekindle the public condemnation and, as Byron told Scott, 'gave great offence at Rome to the respectable 10 or 20,000 English travellers then and there assembled'. Anyone who courted Byron's friendship, such as the Irish traveller and roué, Buck Whaley (1766-1800), risked ostracism themselves. To her credit the great romantic intellectual, Madame de Stael (1766-1817), who was in Switzerland at the time, characteristically ignored public opinion and spoke out in Byron's favour while insisting that he visit her at her house in Coppet as often as possible.

Byron's humiliation at the hands of English society and the London press did not end with his departure from England. In Geneva English tourists hired telescopes to spy on him across the lake at the house where he was staying. When he arrived in Rome and was exploring the roof of St Peter's, he encountered an old acquaintance, Lady Liddell, and was shocked to hear her order her daughter to avert her eyes as he passed saying 'do not look at him, he is dangerous to look at'. Such rejection seems to have provoked a powerful reaction in the poet. 'It is odd' he wrote 'but agitation or contest of any kind gives a rebound to my spirits.' Now anger and sorrow at what he saw as the vindictive injustice of his banishment drove him into a new phase of creative and heterosexual energy.

In his first year in Venice, he told John Murray that as well as his passionate affair with Teresa Guiccioli, he had sexual relations with more than 200 women of all classes. It was as if by this display of heterosexuality he was seeking to counter the rumours that continued to emanate from England. There his wife and half-sister seemed determined to prove to each other that Byron was insane. Although his sister's letters were discussed in minute detail by both women, they appear to contain no reference to his attraction to boys, for Byron had learned the bitter lesson of keeping his mouth shut on such matters. His actions were a different matter and the poet Shelley informed a friend that not only was Lord Byron familiar with the lowest sort of woman picked up in his gondola, but that he was also associating 'with wretches who seem almost to have lost the gait and physiognomy of man and who do not scruple to avow practices which are not only not named but I believe seldom conceived in England.' Clearly this suggests that Byron, whether sexually involved or not, was consorting with effeminate men or transvestites. Few men appear to have been more superficially self-confident than Byron, although one of his biographers, Louis Crompton, claims that he possessed a great deal of underlying insecurity in his flamboyant behaviour combined with a deep sense of guilt for his compulsive whoring at Cambridge, his incest with his sister, his cold and disdainful treatment of his wife, but most of all for his homosexual feelings.

Within a few years of commencing his exile, two dramatic events occurred in England that bore a strange relevance to Byron's decision to leave. First, the Bishop of Clogher, the son of the Irish peer, the Earl of Roden, was arrested for having sex with a soldier in a common alehouse in Westminster. As the diarist Charles Greville recalled, the bishop 'made a desperate resistance when taken and if his breeches had not been down they think he might have got away.' When bailed, the bishop fled the country and the soldier absconded in similar circumstances a few weeks later. A coarse, if amusing, rhyme began to be heard on the London streets: 'The Bishop in order to mock the Church went out to fish for a bugger. He baited his hook with a soldier's arse and hauled up the Bishop of Clogher.' *The Times* fulminated against this 'monstrous depravity' and seemed satisfied that the Bishop had 'quitted forever the country which his presence had polluted'. What so outraged the press was that in 1810 the bishop's coachman had been charged with spreading false rumours about his master's sexuality and had been transported for life. The furore that the scandal provoked explains to some degree the reluctance of some of Byron's friends to stand by him.

Three weeks after the Bishop's departure, a far more prominent figure became the victim of a similar, if unproven, sexual scandal. Robert Stewart, the Foreign Secretary and Marquis of Londonderry (1769–1822), had been the target of several of Byron's most vitriolic attacks in the House of Lords. When news of the bizarre scandal surrounding the Bishop of Clogher became public, it seemed to galvanize Lord Londonderry into a morbid fear that a similar fate awaited him. This was not mere paranoia as he had told friends that he was being blackmailed for a similar crime himself. A few months earlier he had visited a brothel and had, so he claimed, found that the woman provided was in fact a man in woman's clothing and that he ran panic-stricken from the house. The perpetrators of this odd charade threatened to reveal the details to his wife, began to appear outside his house and sent him letters demanding money. It is hard to believe that the revelation of an encounter with an ordinary female prostitute would have caused Londonderry such anxiety. It is more likely that he feared social ruin in the manner of William Beckford and Lord Byron for his 'unnatural' predilections. Unable because of his government office to flee the country as the free-spirited Byron had, he became borne down by guilt. When a few days later he had to visit George IV at Windsor on state business, he claimed that he had been accused of the same crime as the Bishop of Clogher and that he intended to flee the country. The King was shocked by this bizarre self-accusation but he urged the distraught man to calm himself, to go home and rest at his country seat at North Cray in Kent. There, his wife, forewarned from London, summoned the local physician, who saw at once that Londonderry was in a suicidal mood and ordered her to remove and lock up her husband's pistols and all sharp instruments. The next morning something about his demeanour so alarmed his wife that she summoned the doctor again while leaving her husband to dress. While left alone Londonderry went through to his dressing room, found a small penknife that he had hidden and, at the very moment that the doctor entered the room, he slashed the carotid artery in his neck.

Lord Londonderry had paid a far higher price than Byron for the accusations he endured, although he was far more vulnerable to blackmail than the poet. Politically ruthless in helping suppress the Irish Rising of 1798 and a key member of the contemporary Tory government, he was the natural political enemy of Lord Byron. Yet, fate had forced him to confront the same accusations of sexual deviance as Byron. To such a man the sense of shame and guilt would have been overwhelming. Strangely, given his own brush with public attitudes towards homosexuality, Byron spared neither the Bishop of Clogher nor the Foreign Secretary in his scathing criticism. In the poem 'Don Juan', written soon after the event but not published until after his death, Byron is even more acerbic about the late Lord Londonderry dismissing him as 'an intellectual eunuch, Cold-blooded, smooth-faced, placid miscreant / The vulgarest tool that Tyranny could want.'

News of Londonderry's death reached Byron at a time when he was tiring of his relationship with Teresa Guiccioli. For a man of his temperament the greatest enemy had always been boredom. When the London Greek Committee contacted him in April 1823 to act as its agent in aiding the Greek war for independence from the Turks, Byron responded with alacrity. He may well have seen it as an opportunity to return to the heroic yearnings of his youth and a Greece where brave men driven by an ideal of freedom came together as comrades to drive out the tyrant. After careful planning, Byron left Genoa in Italy on 2 August onboard a chartered ship, arriving at the Ionian island of Cephalonia, where he set up camp in Metaxata. There he arranged for a large sum of his money to be sent from London to prepare the fledgling Greek fleet for battle.

On landing at Cephalonia, Byron gave aid to a Greek refugee widow and her 15-year-old son, Loukas Chalandritsanos. This unusually attractive boy most probably sparked memories of John Eddleston – certainly Byron fell desperately in love with him. When he set sail at the end of December to join the Greek leader Prince Alexandros Mavrokordatos (1791–1865) on the Western Greek mainland at Missolonghi, Byron took Loukas with him. The strategy agreed by the Greek leaders was to attack the Turkish-held fortress of Lepanto and attempt to unite the factious forces of eastern and western Greece. On the voyage from Cephalonia, Byron suffered an uncharacteristic bout of nervousness and became convinced that the ship would be attacked by Turks and carry off Loukas. In that event, the poet wrote dramatically, 'I would rather cut him in pieces myself than have him taken out by those barbarians.' Byron was now completely devoted to Loukas and when the boy contracted a fever in Missolonghi, the poet gave him his own bed to sleep on and nursed him back to health. Loukas, although eager to accept Byron's gifts and money, does not appear to have fully returned his patron's passion, causing Byron to become increasingly irritated.

This unrequited passion led to Byron writing his last cycle of poems – 'Love and Death' – which begin with the words 'On This Day I Complete My Thirty Sixth Year'. In them, the poet laments that he is in love with someone who cannot love him in return. More autobiographical than anything he had previously written, Byron chronicles his despairing love and the occasions when Loukas's welfare had caused him so much worry. The poem ends with Byron's sad admission that Lukas does not – and cannot – love him 'though it be my lot / To strongly – wrongly – vainly – love thee still'. Once again Byron was facing humiliation and rejection. It is no wonder that in the poem he pledges to 'tread these reviving passions down' and devote himself to the heroic struggle for Greek freedom on the battlefield. Remarkably, the poem, although published shortly after his death, was not taken as a declaration of love for Lukas until 70 years after its appearance in print. The reason being that John Cam Hobhouse had left a note, purportedly by Byron himself, saying that it referred 'to no one in particular' and was 'a mere poetical Scherzo', even though Loukas is referred to in each of the six stanzas.

On 15 February 1824, Lord Byron fell ill with fever. The conventional remedy of bleeding with unsterilized instruments not only weakened him further, but almost certainly led to the sepsis that caused the death on 19 April of England's most famous exile of the age and her most illustrious romantic poet. When news of Byron's death at Missolonghi reached London, Hobhouse who had not read them, insisted that the pages of Byron's unpublished memoirs be burned to preserve his reputation. Both John Murray, Byron's publisher, and his biographer Thomas Moore agreed, and what might well have been one of the most precious documents of the century was consigned to the flames. When Byron's corpse was returned to England, his friends had hoped for a hero's welcome for him that would include a state funeral in Westminster Abbey in London, and a prominent place in Poets' Corner. But the Dean of Westminster adamantly refused and the body of the dead poet was instead interred in the family tomb in Nottinghamshire.

However, when Byron's coffin passed up the River Thames on 5 July, both banks were lined with spectators. Byron's body lay on view in a private house in Great George Street in Westminster for two days and the public was admitted entrance by ticket. In the face of official disapproval, there were displays of near hysterical emotion for a man who was widely admired in spite of his faults, as one of the first modern celebrities. Although most of the crowd was composed of the reading public, many working men were also present, drawn by Byron's uncompromising condemnation of tyranny and injustice. His supposed moral failings and in particular his rumoured homosexuality appeared completely irrelevant at a time like this. Soon the police had to be called to control the sheer numbers and wooden barriers were erected round the coffin to protect it from the crush.

In contrast to his ignominious journey into exile, Lord Byron's return was a triumph that confirmed the birth of the imperishable Byron legend. The *Morning Chronicle* newspaper reported, 'Thus has perished, in the flower of his age, one of the greatest poets England has produced' while the *Morning Herald* declared that 'The poetical literature of England has lost one of its brightest ornaments, and the age decidedly its greatest genius.' The working-class poet John Clare, who watched Byron's funeral procession as it passed down a packed Oxford Street in London, wrote prophetically in his journal that evening 'The common people felt his merits and his power and the common people of a country are the best feelings of a prophesy of futurity'.

EDWARD LEAR'S ESCAPE TO FANTASY

When news of Lord Byron's premature death first arrived in England it caused the 11-year-old Edward Lear to burst into tears. Byron was his childhood hero and Lear wrote in his diary that in the days following he used to 'sit in the cold looking at the stars ... stupefied and crying when I heard that Ld. Byron was dead'.

Like Byron, the future artist and humorist Lear would become an exile travelling to Albania and Greece in the footsteps of his hero. Unlike Byron's privileged upbringing, however, Lear's early life was fraught with hardship and danger, both real and imagined. Once a wealthy stockbroker, his father had fallen on hard times, gone bankrupt and ended up in the King's Bench Prison in Southwark, London. The family were exiled from the comfortable lifestyle they had known and forced to live in shabby rented accommodation in the suburbs of London.

There had always been a shadow hanging over Lear's childhood because he and his elder sister were the only living survivors of the 20 children born to his parents. He was a weak and sickly child and the insecurity that he must have felt from his earliest moments was further intensified by his mother's constant ill health. At the age of 5, Edward Lear was handed over to his sister, Ann, 22 years his elder, to be brought up by her. Although she genuinely loved the boy, she was unable to compensate for the parental rejection that gave a haunted sense of desertion to everything that Lear later wrote.

In 1817 he experienced the first of the persistent but mild epileptic fits that were to dog him for the rest of his life. He referred to these attacks as a visit from 'The Demon' and later as 'The Morbids'. Lear was convinced, like many of his contemporaries, that epilepsy would lead to a deterioration of the brain and early death. This belief was encouraged by the harrowing experience of watching his elder sister Jane suffer numerous seizures before dying long before she reached adulthood. In spite of their devastating effect, he managed to keep the seizures a secret to anyone outside his family. If having to endure these attacks were not enough, Lear also became the victim of one of the many curious medical beliefs circulating in Victorian England that linked moral laxity with divine punishment. In this case, it was the absurd theory that epileptic fits were caused by masturbation. Lear found it impossible to exercise self-control and so was condemned to a lifetime of guilt and remorse. Only towards the end of his life when medical research had become more enlightened did Edward Lear begin to suspect that he had been deceived. Lear's famous rhyme about the Pobble who had no nose may well have a link to this early trauma, as did his tendency in later life to run away from problems.

The trauma of a Victorian childhood dominated by early death and moral strictures that trapped many artists in a state of suspended moral animation was not unusual. Lear's biographer, Jackie Wullschläger, has explored this phenomenon not only with Lear but also in the lives of other near-contemporary authors of children's fantasies, such as Lewis Carroll (1832–98), J. M. Barrie (1860–1937), Kenneth Grahame (1859–1932) and A. A. Milne (1882–1956). She believes that each of them relied on the presence of a child as a muse or catalyst to trigger their adult imagination into creating an extraordinary fantasy. She points out that as well as all having a peculiarly strong affinity with childhood they also 'shared a reluctance to engage in conventional behaviour and relationships'.

Growing up at that time was certainly a serious business for boys like Lear for the Evangelical church exercised a pernicious and puritanical control of large sections of the community. In such a world levity was as abhorrent as homosexuality and merriment a stage on the road to perdition. Lear attempted his own modest act of rebellion through his verses, showing that life could be humorous, and even once told a little girl, 'My dear child, I'm sure we shall be allowed to laugh in Heaven!'

Although psychologically and morally oppressed, Lear displayed a precocious talent for art and at the age of just 15 he started earning a living by producing posters and display material for local shops and making detailed anatomical sketches for London hospitals. Recognition of his talent came when he was commissioned by the newly established Zoological Gardens in London's Regent's Park to produce the illustrations for a book on parrots. The result was one of the finest series of animal drawings ever produced in England and led to his appointment as art master to the young Queen Victoria (1819–1901; Queen of the United Kingdom of Great Britain and Ireland 1837–1901). This success led to other commissions including the Earl of Derby's invitation in 1832 for Lear to draw the animals in his menagerie at Knowsley Hall in Lancashire. At the end of each day's work, Lear would play in the nursery with the Earl's children. These daily encounters proved the inspiration for the nonsense verses that would be an even greater legacy than his art. The fantastic creatures of Lear's imagination were as humorous as they were appealing and into their creation Lear poured all the rage and frustration produced by the social constraints he had endured. Many of these characters are eccentrics in conflict with society, who risk being shunned for their oddity.

Lear was – like many of his literary creations – odd in appearance with a bald head, pebble glasses and a misshapen nose. His drawings of himself are revelatory and almost as strange as any of his imagined creatures, acknowledging himself as a misfit with a long nose, bushy beard and spindly legs. There is also in his characters an attempt to escape into the anonymity he sought for himself. Some do not even have a name but are formally described as 'a Person', 'a Man' or 'a Lady' and are only distinguished by their unusual appearance, peculiar behaviour or outlandish dress. What happens to the characters in Lear's rhymes is the direct result of their distinctive oddity, thus making them the victims of their own idiosyncrasy. As Wullschläger has written 'Only someone self-educated, living beyond mainstream English cultural life, sensing himself to be an outsider, would have had the boldness and freedom to write as he did, yet the psychological cost was enormous.'

At Knowsley Hall, Lear found the acceptance and the sheltered environment that suited his withdrawn personality. Lear might well have remained at Knowsley had not his health suddenly deteriorated in the spring of 1837. Apart from the occupational hazard of eyestrain, he was also suffering from persistent bronchitis and asthma. The new Earl of Derby and his nephew Robert Hornby kindly offered to pay Lear's expenses if he agreed to travel Rome to recover his health. Lear accepted eagerly and set off at the end of July that year. Part of his motivation in leaving England was, like Lord Byron's, to escape the sexually conformist and censorious society of England. However, whereas Byron's sexuality had been dynamic and unconventional, Lear's was timid and repressed. Although freed from the inhibitions of respectable English society, Lear could never bring himself to openly recognize the strong homosexual desires that he expressed in many of his letters and diaries. In this way Lear was typical of his age, as men and women with similar tendencies took great pains to disguise or even sublimate them. In Victorian England it was essential for men to conform to a conventional marriage even if they were deeply unhappy in such a union. Those who did not were considered by themselves, as well as by society, as not only odd but also weak or even mentally ill.

When Lear arrived in Italy, three months later, he found himself in a far more liberal and relaxed society. For the next half century, he would wander across southern Europe and the Middle East, finally reaching India in search of spectacular landscapes to paint. Apart from a long sojourn in England between 1849 and 1853, and a few other short visits back, Edward Lear was to spend the rest of his life in exile as he established a reputation as one of the finest topographical landscape painters of the 19th century. Occasionally he thought of returning home and marrying a woman who would care for him and alleviate his loneliness. Indeed, on one occasion in 1866 he even came close to making this idea a reality with the

Honourable Augusta Bethell, a young woman he had known since her childhood. Cautious as ever, Lear unwisely consulted her sister and was firmly discouraged from pursuing the matter, although he later discovered that Augusta would gladly have accepted him at the time. Perhaps in an attempt to exorcise the unhappy episode, he incorporated it into the nonsense rhyme of 'The Yonghy-Bonghy-Bo' and his hilarious but forlorn courtship of Lady Jingly Jones.

Emotionally drawn to men, Lear continued to pretend that he wanted to marry and live the conventional life of a Victorian gentleman. In reality, fulfilment might have come if he had accepted the demands of his own nature but he remained constantly on the move, wandering from one place to another. The emotional relationships he did form were invariably with men and all appear to have been platonic. The most important of these were with Chichester Fortescue (1823–98), later Lord Carlingford, and Thomas Baring (1826–1904), later Lord Northbrook. Both were great admirers of Lear's unique talents and corresponded freely with him for many years. Occasionally one or other would join him on a painting expedition to an exotic location and share the companionship as well as the hardships of the journey.

When Lear met another future peer, Franklin Lushington (d.1901), in Malta in 1848, he fell completely in love with him. It became the one relationship that would seriously test Lear's determination to remain safely asexual. Lushington was a young barrister on holiday from London and he agreed to tour southern Greece with his mentor in what were certainly the happiest weeks of Lear's life. This could have been the cathartic moment in Lear's emotional life but Lushington kept his distance and made it plain that Lear had misjudged the situation. 'He is so changed since I first knew him, while I have remained so absurdly the same', Lear wrote sadly to his friend Emily Tennyson. The rejection, however, never succeeded in diminishing the genuine love that the older man felt. When Lushington became seriously ill in 1855, Lear was so grief-stricken that he wrote to the family offering to come and comfort them. Although they remained friends until Lear's death, the disparity of their feelings for one other was to constantly torment Lear and only abated when Lushington made the conventional marriage that had eluded Lear. The arrival of Lushington's children allowed Lear to transfer his emotions from the father to the children, enabling him to play the part of amusing uncle.

Late in life, Lear developed a passion for another much younger man, Hubert Congreve, who he had met in Italy. Congreve had artistic talent and gave Lear the hope that the young man would come and live with him, in the Renaissance manner, and be his apprentice. Again his feelings were not reciprocated and, perhaps realizing that he had left it too late to form a deep attachment with either a man or a woman, Lear broke down and wept when Congreve finally left him in San Remo to return to England. It was in northern Italy, after a near lifetime of travel, that, in 1871, Edward Lear came finally to settle on the Italian Riviera. At first he lived alone, but was then joined by his faithful Suliot manservant, Giorgio Kokali, who was to stay with him for 25 years.

Although Franklin Lushington destroyed most of Lear's papers after his death in 1888, one surviving diary contains an intriguing entry that might explain Lear's fear of physical contact with other men. He records the death of a cousin who 50 years earlier 'did me the greatest Evil done to me in life, excepting that done by C – and which must last now to the end – spite of all reason and effort.' Biographers have speculated that this refers to a sexual advance or even an assault on the 10-year-old Edward by his 19-year-old cousin, Frederick Harding.

Some psychologists have recognized in Lear's refusal to either acknowledge his homosexuality or attempt a heterosexual marriage the signs of the phenomenon of the 'eternal boy', someone who remains too long in an adolescent psychology of a 17- or 18-year-old youth. This state is often associated with too great a dependence on the mother and the result is often a man who is either a homosexual or a seducer of women unable to commit himself to one person. Lear appears typical of this type, suffering the constant fear of being pinned down by either a person or a place. The morally conservative climate fostered by the Evangelical church that existed during his lifetime added to Lear's problems. Its stress on the sanctity of family life, the value of conventional behaviour, the repression of sins of the flesh and even the upholding of Britain's imperial mission all created a climate hostile to any manifestation of sexual and social unorthodoxy, especially homosexuality. The Evangelicals opposed nearly everything that was lighthearted or fun, particularly indulgence in alcohol or sex. It has been said that Lear's fraught upbringing had one beneficial effect in that it allowed him to exist outside mainstream English cultural life. As an outsider he was able to write in his own distinctive anarchic voice using nonsense and humour to undermine the conformity of the age.

Others in Victorian society troubled by powerful sexual drives but lacking Lear's outlet of humour had to find an alternative form of release. One manifestation of this in literature is Robert Louis Stevenson's (1850–94) novel, *The Strange Case of Dr Jekyll and Mr Hyde*, which was published in 1886. Stevenson's novel can be interpreted as a Victorian version of the Greek myth of Narcissus and it has been suggested that the author used his literary creation as a release mechanism for his own repressed homosexuality, with Mr Hyde representing the primeval sexuality that Dr Jekyll has previously managed to control. In one scene in the book, Jekyll is lying in bed when he is visited by Hyde, who compels him to rise and do his bidding by proxy. A similar relationship based on narcissism is the central theme of Oscar Wilde's *The Picture of Dorian Gray*, another classic of Victorian horror literature dealing with thinly disguised homoeroticism. Realizing that his beauty will one day fade, Dorian sells his soul in a Faustian pact ensuring that his portrait will age and fade rather than his physical self. However, as Dorian is increasingly forced into acts of debauchery his portrait changes to reflect the hideousness of his actions.

When examined closely, these works of horror fiction reflect an attempt at a fantasy escape from a life constrained by powerful moral pressures and religious conformity. They also make Edward's Lear's quiet journey into exile and nonsense far less isolated and far more credible. The great pity is that his life did not achieve a final resolution. In his last poem, 'Incidents in the Life of My Uncle Arly', the hero wanders over hills and dales to gaze at 'golden sunsets blazing' and finds a first-class railway ticket, a metaphor for Lear's invitation to join upper-class Victorian society. However, like his creator, Uncle Arly's 'shoes were far too tight' – he cannot fit in and roams away rather like the lonely and unresolved Lear.

THE QUEST FOR CORVO

Some other men with homosexual drives were luckier than Edward Lear. Those with enough courage and sufficient financial resources did not hesitate to turn their backs on their own repressive society and join the colonies of English and German exiles attracted by the moral liberalism of Italy. If they were reasonably discreet in their behaviour, they could enjoy the pleasures of the sun, the sea and an intimate association with local boys.

In 1878 at Taormina in eastern Sicily, Baron Wilhelm von Gloeden (1856–1931) began a pleasant exile from his native Germany photographing the magnificent views of Mount Etna. There, he took his celebrated compositions of naked youths draped in classical poses over the statues and broken columns of the ancient Greek and Roman remains. In order to justify the models' nudity, von Gloeden claimed that his pictures should be seen as the most authentic way to illustrate the works of Homer and Theocritus. As his photographic assistant, von Gloeden hired a 14-year-old boy with dark skin and large eyes called Pancrazio Bucini, who he nicknamed 'Il Moro' – the Moor. The boy became his model and lover. What is unusual about von Gloeden's activities is that he did not exploit the ignorance or poverty of his models and insisted on a system of accounts that provided royalties to all those who had posed for him. These earnings allowed many local young men to get an education, start a business or purchase their own fishing boat. In a further act of generosity, he secretly provided dowries for the daughters of poor families engaged to his young male models.

By 1900 Baron Wilhelm von Gloeden had become famous as a photographer of classical male nudes and his work was circulating beyond gay aesthetes to a wider audience through the new magazines associated with the German *Körperkultur* movement that idealized health, exercise and nudism. His reputation attracted many celebrities to Sicily, among them Oscar Wilde who, just released from prison, presented his host with a signed copy of 'The Ballad of Reading Gaol'. As the Ladies of Llangollen had discovered, the privacy of exile could be frustrated by unwelcome fame and the constant interruption of visitors. One uninvited guest was Kaiser Wilhelm II of Germany (1859–1941; German emperor 1888–1918), who on several occasions anchored the Imperial Yacht at Taormina and joined von Gloeden at his villa to spend a night with one of the boys. The views of Mount Etna were as much an attraction as the possibility of a brief liaison, for among other visitors were Alfonso XII of Spain (1857–85; King of Spain 1874–85), the King of Siam and Edward VII of England (1841–1910; King of Great Britain and Ireland 1901–1910), who carried some of von Gloeden's nude photos back to London hidden in his diplomatic bag. Von Gloeden's network of friends and acquaintances was extraordinarily diverse and included wealthy bankers and industrialists, such as the Rothschilds, the Stönnes, the Morgans and the Vanderbilts. The composer Richard Strauss (1864–1949) and the writers André Gide (1869–1951), Anatole France (1844–1924), Rudyard Kipling (1865–1936) and Gabriele d'Annunzio (1863–1938) often joined his cosmopolitan guest list. Gide, in particular, was much taken with the beauty of the villa and while there wrote his great novel *The Immoralist*, which explores a married man's discovery of his homosexuality.

Meanwhile Pancrazio Bucini, having married and had children, took over the running of the estate and the management of von Gloeden's vast picture collection as the photographer passed into old age. Politics had little relevance to this small corner of Sicily but in 1929 an alliance was formed between the Vatican and Italy's fascist government and in an attempt to suppress supposed immorality the police began taking an interest in von Gloeden. A raid on the villa was carried out and more than 1,000 glass negatives and 2,000 prints were confiscated or destroyed. The situation deteriorated further in 1936 when Bucini found the police hammering on his door at night and they carried away most of what was left of the precious glass negatives. In spite of Bucini's pleas, many were smashed before their custodian was taken off to jail. At his trial Bucini strongly defended himself and the baron, who had died five years previously, against the charges of pornography. He passionately defended the life and art of von Gloeden, claiming that the court did not have the competence to judge such works of art. He went on to list the names of the many eminent collectors, museums and institutions, including the Italian Ministry of Education, that were all proud to display the baron's work. Moved by the patent honesty of this simple man, the judges did not bow to political pressure and voted in Bucini's favour. What remained of von Gloeden's work was released and even today postcards showing his nude Sicilian youths can still be bought at Taormina.

While von Gloeden was at the height of his fame in Sicily the French aesthete and photographer, Count Jacques d'Adelswird Fersen (1880-1923) was building himself a lavish villa on the Isle of Capri. Fersen, whose family owned some of the largest steel mills in France, had been accused in 1903 of holding black masses at his house in Paris. These had reportedly been attended by local schoolboys who indulged in sexual misconduct with the owner. When the case came to court, Fersen was convicted of indecent behaviour with minors and sentenced to six months in prison, fined 50 francs and deprived of his civil rights for five years. Many Parisians thought the scandal to be their own version of the Oscar Wilde affair that had occurred in London a few years earlier. Like Wilde, Fersen decided he could not face the social ignominy that awaited him outside prison and exiled himself on the Isle of Capri.

The discovery of the stunningly beautiful Blue Grotto there in 1826 and the island's past association with the Emperor Tiberius (42 BC–AD 37) gave it a particular cachet for gay libertines. Here Tiberius had frolicked in old age with his own minions, boy slaves who were supposed to have swum around him in the pool nibbling at his genitals like fish. Apart from the beauty of the setting, Fersen was delighted to discover Capri had a ready availability of poor but handsome young boys willing to participate in his theatrical recreations of Greek life. Fersen's *tableaux vivants* could be easily captured on film although a complex setting made them differ from von Gloeden's less contrived pictures. What resulted was a series of images of naked young boys draped decorously on or around ruined temples and statuary from the age of Tiberius. Wary lest his activities arouse the interest of the local police, Fersen always produced two versions of each print, one for tourists showing his models partially clad and the other revealing them fully naked. The latter would be put aside for sale to visiting homosexuals, such as Oscar Wilde who bought a selection. Together with von Gloeden's pictures, Fersen's images are probably the first known attempts at mild homosexual pornography. However, his attempt in 1903 to publish a pioneering journal devoted to pederastic love was still too controversial and the project ended in failure.

News of Fersen's activities on the island added to Capri's growing attraction as a refuge from homophobia – by the end of the 19th century making it an ideal retreat for a new generation of wealthy homosexuals. One such visitor drawn to the island was Friedrich 'Fritz' Krupp (1854–1902), heir to the largest privately owned industrial and munitions company in Germany. Having proved himself a competent administrator in the family business, Fritz Krupp, rather like the Japanese Emperor during the Second World War (1939–45), showed a far greater preference for marine biology than administration. The stress caused by his father's insistence that he marry young, produce an heir and take his place at the head of the Krupp industrial empire led to the young man having a serious physical and mental breakdown. During a period of convalescence he was sent off on what was to prove a fateful visit to Italy. Once free of paternal control, he stayed away as long as possible, basing himself on Capri and began studying the oceanography that had always fascinated him. An attraction of a far different sort arose when Krupp began to take notice of the handsome local boys. By 1898, he had virtually exiled himself from Germany and taken up full-time residence on the island, finding intellectual fulfilment in his science and emotional satisfaction in homosexual relationships. For the first time in his life he appeared emotionally at peace and this new contentment inspired him to become a generous benefactor to the local community who in turn made him an honorary citizen.

Fritz Krupp's love life raised many eyebrows but produced few objections from his generously rewarded neighbours in Italy. However, pressure from Berlin was never far away and his father began to insist that he return to Berlin more frequently to play his part in company life. To ensure that these tiresome visits were more agreeable, Fritz arranged for several of his young Caprian friends to travel ahead of him to Berlin and pose as temporary staff at the Hotel Bristol. Whenever he arrived these men would be waiting to indulge his whims and share his bed. The inevitable gossip among the staff soon spread to the hotel guests who complained indignantly to the manager of the commotion coming from Herr Krupp's suite.

Dislike of the ruthless Krupps was one of the legacies of Prussian aggression towards its neighbours and nowhere was this more intense than in Italy. When news of Fritz's gay activities at the Hotel Bristol reached the Italian press in 1902, it was eager to expose him. Even more compromising than the rumours in the Italian press were photographs of the homosexual parties, copies of which had been passed to the Berlin Chief of Police. Scandalous tales of all-male orgies at Krupp's villa on Capri began to appear in both German and Italian newspapers. Ignorant of her husband's true sexual tastes, Fritz's wife Margaretha was so shocked that she suffered a mental collapse and had to be admitted to an asylum. Within a month specific accusations of sodomy were being made. Fritz had no option but to sue for libel or face the social ruin that similarly overwhelmed William Beckford, Lord Byron and Oscar Wilde. Invited to discuss the matter with an important family friend, Kaiser Wilhelm, Krupp could not bring himself to face the embarrassing interview and on the morning of 22 November 1902, killed himself. No autopsy was made and his body was placed immediately in a sealed casket. Italy had proved to be both Fritz Krupp's salvation and his nemesis and a similar fate was to overtake another exiled homosexual a decade later.

Exile in Italy was to prove as futile a quest for happiness for the eccentric English writer Frederick Rolfe (1860–1913) as it had been for Fritz Krupp. Better known by his pen name of Baron Corvo, Rolfe was an extraordinary character whose unique talent as a writer was frustrated throughout his life by a contentious, unreasonable and aggressive character. Born to a Dissenting family at Cheapside in London in July 1860, Rolfe was a precocious child so obsessed with religious symbols that at the age 14 he had a cross tattooed on his breast. Although he never completed a formal education, he did acquire an excellent self-taught knowledge of the classics, theology and history that enabled him to bluff his way into a teaching post at Grantham Grammar School in Lincolnshire. There, in an action that was to determine the rest of his life, he converted to Roman Catholicism. From the moment that he received his First Communion at the hands of another famous convert, Cardinal Manning, he determined to become a priest. Rolfe persuaded the Bishop of Shrewsbury to sponsor his studies at the leading Catholic seminary of St Mary's College near Birmingham. There began the strange pattern of wilful and counterproductive behaviour that would make him his own worst enemy. Challenging authority became his special forte and rather than attending classes he spent much of his time painting pictures with religious themes and ignoring his teachers' constant appeals to conform. Inevitably, the Principal grew tired of his behaviour and asked him to leave. In the months after quitting the college, Rolfe revealed his latent homosexuality by writing a series of emotional poems, among them 'Ballade of Boys Bathing', which contains the openly homoerotic lines:

White Boys, ruddy, and tanned, and bare
With lights and shadows of rose and grey
And the sea like pearls in their shining hair
The boys who bathe in Saint Andrews Bay

For the rest of his life close friendships with boys and violent quarrels with adults would characterize his behaviour.

Still determined to become a priest in spite of this early setback, Rolfe with his customary self-confidence managed to get himself admitted to Scots College in Rome. Unfortunately, he repeated the same mistakes he made at St Mary's, repeatedly missing lectures and concentrating on his own interests, particularly on writing poems that he sent to various magazines in London. Once again it was his arrogance and open disdain for the teachers, as well as for his fellow novitiates, that really brought about his downfall. After having evaded every attempt to persuade him to leave quietly, Rolfe, who had taken to his bed in defiance, was lifted bodily by the college staff and together with his mattress deposited ignominiously on the Roman pavement outside. This second expulsion from a Catholic seminary effectively ended any further hope of his becoming a priest. Utterly insensitive to the trouble he had caused he described this last dramatic ejection as his 'life's great disappointment'. For the next few years he behaved as if the rejection had never happened and continued wearing the regulation clothes and behaving in the same pious manner as a trainee priest. Ever the optimist Rolfe was convinced that he would eventually triumph. However, this unlikely prospect receded even further when he began an onslaught of vituperative letters to the principals of both colleges that had expelled him.

The latent paranoia in Rolfe's character was revealed as he became convinced that his downfall was the result of a papal conspiracy against him rather than the product of his own behaviour. These paranoid delusions were outlined in detail in a barrage of letters written to his remaining Catholic friends. Rolfe's complete inability to be objective about himself or to deal fairly with others condemned him to a form of personal exile in society wherever he went. His latent homosexuality further distanced him from conventional society, while his irrepressible obnoxiousness made intimacy with potential male lovers equally difficult. Constantly short of money, Rolfe showed complete ingratitude for any generosity shown him. New friends were soon disillusioned by what appeared to be his total selfishness regarding any gift or loan made to him. While in Rome he had developed the habit of obtaining credit from tradesmen. He only survived by the charity of an aristocratic lady who gave him a room in her palace in Rome. There he began to study Renaissance history and take photographs of local boys in the manner of Count Fersen, later immortalizing them as characters in his book *Stories Toto Told Me*, published in 1898. In spite of the poverty this was the happiest time of his life as he lazed in the sunshine and explored the Alban Hills around Rome. This, like all the imagined idylls in Rolfe's life, ended in a bitter return to reality when in November 1890 poverty forced him to return to England.

Rolfe arrived back at Christchurch in Hampshire with the assumed name of Frederick, Baron Corvo, claiming that his Italian patroness had conferred the title on him. It was to be the pen name he used in all subsequent writings. Still desperately short of money, he gained a commission to paint a fresco in a church at Christchurch. To create the religious figures he used a selection of the nude photographs of boys that he had taken in Italy. A friend recalled walking into the church and finding Rolfe projecting these risqué images onto the wet plaster of the wall with a magic lantern in order to draw the outlines for his religious figures. One was the centrepiece for a mural of the Ascension of Christ and showed a particularly handsome youth of about 17 with flaxen hair and blue eyes caught in mid-air as he leapt into the Lake of Nemi. Rolfe continued with the photographic studies of young boys he had begun in Italy. They may have raised some local eyebrows in rural Hampshire but Rolfe's friends seemed blissfully unconcerned by his homoerotic activities. One neighbour generously provided his own young son as a model, helping Rolfe arrange the naked boy wearing only a knitted cap in a series of classical poses.

Rolfe became convinced that his future lay as a professional photographer and having experienced all that Christchurch could offer he moved to London. Eventually he found a position in a photographic studio but inevitably he became involved in a dispute with the owner and found himself ejected from the premises by the police. Ironically, in the short time that he was there he displayed a genuine talent for photography, inventing one of the first practical underwater photography techniques that was later taken up by the Royal Navy. This was the very essence of Rolfe's tragedy; here was a man of great talent, brimming with originality and good ideas but whose uncontrollably fractious character invariably led to frustration and defeat. Moving on to Scotland in 1894, Rolfe was now so poor that he was unable to pay for his lodgings. According to a local newspaper report, he was ejected from the premises wearing only his pyjamas and 'shot onto the pavement as he stood ... his clothing was thrown after him, which he ultimately donned.' He was destitute and was forced to swallow his pride and resort to accepting the help of a local charity, the Association for Improving the Condition of the Poor in Aberdeen. He brazenly began writing begging letters to the great and the good in society including William Waldorf Astor (1848–1919) and the Duke of Norfolk. Most were ignored but one met with remarkable success for Rolfe's boldness had intrigued another maverick, the wealthy socialist MP Henry Champion.

Recognizing a man who was as iconoclastic as himself, Champion offered Rolfe a well-paid job as journalist on his radical newspaper *The Aberdeen Standard*. A more stable and prosperous future seemed imminent only for Rolfe's hopes to be dashed by the sudden departure of Champion for Australia. Not only had Champion lost much of his fortune in a business swindle but he had also been expelled from the Labour Party in disgrace. Plunged into penury once more, Rolfe decided to leave Scotland and try his luck in Wales, where he had other contacts. By letter he had applied to restore a bronze sculpture at the Capuchin monastery at Pantasaph, using a special resin of his own invention. All he asked in return for the work was free board and lodging but the priest in charge having agreed the deal then reneged on it. Craftily he persuaded Rolfe to write down the formula then gave it to a fellow priest to make up while refusing to honour his side of the bargain. Bitter and more disillusioned than ever Rolfe trudged off to the nearby Catholic shrine of Holywell, where he persuaded yet another priest, Father Beauclerk to allow him to paint banners for his church, again in return for board and lodging. Once more his good intentions were sabotaged by his own compulsive and offensive behaviour, provoking Beauclerk to such fury that he cancelled the project and ordered Rolfe out of the church. Unable to acknowledge his own responsibility for yet another fiasco, Rolfe held the priest wholly to blame and presented him with an exorbitant bill of £700 for work already completed. This was the start of an ill-tempered dispute that dragged on for the next 10 years during the course of which Rolfe accused the priest of being a 'habitual wanton and malignant liar, a calumniator, a curser, a thief.'

In spite of the mayhem of Rolfe's daily life, he persisted in his search for employment while at the same time developing his talent as a writer. His writing, in contrast to his life at this time, reveals a perfectionist with a distinctive, erudite and adventurous prose style. This characteristic style was apparent in his first successful books *Stories Toto Told Me* and *In His Own Image*, which was published in 1901. Other works followed including several accounts of saints' lives supposedly narrated in dialect by a precocious servant. Largely neglected in his lifetime, these works later developed a following because of their unusual homoerotic content. By 1904, Rolfe's promise as writer was fully realized in what was to be his masterpiece, *Hadrian the Seventh*. This ambitious book was written in an even more elaborate prose style and tells the story of George Rose, an expelled seminarian who rises to become pope and when about to transform the world for the better is abruptly assassinated by a fanatical socialist. The whole work is a classic example of wish fulfilment and could only have been the creation of a deeply frustrated man. Graham Greene (1904–91) described it as a 'novel of genius' and it is now widely acclaimed as a 20th-century classic, never once being out of print since the first edition. As early as 1925, D. H. Lawrence (1885–1930) had also recognized its merits calling it a seminal book 'that if the work of a demon as Corvo's contemporaries had claimed then it is the book of a man demon, not a mere poseur. And if some of it is caviar, at least it came out of the belly of a live fish.'

Unaware of his future importance as a writer and worn down by the constant struggle to make a living, Rolfe gave up the struggle in

1. Benvenuto Cellini, (1500–71)

2. Thomas Gray, (1716–71)

3. Henry III (1551–89; king of France 1574–89)

*4. The Ladies of Llangollen: Eleanor Butler (1739–1829)
and Sarah Ponsonby (1755–1831)*

5. William Beckford (1760–1844)

6. Lord Byron (1788–1824)

7. L–R: Edward Lear (1812–88) with Chichester Fortescue
(1823–98), the British Secretary of State for Ireland.

8. John Addington Symonds (1840–93)

9. Oscar Wilde (1854–1900)

10. L–R: W. H. Auden (1907–73) and
Christopher Isherwood (1904–86)

11. Henry James (1843–1916)

12. Gertrude Stein (1874–1946), pictured with her famous portrait by Spanish artist Pablo Picasso (1881–1973)

13. James Baldwin (1924–87)

August 1908 and decided that he had finally exhausted the patience of his erstwhile English friends and was heartily sick of the 'ingratitude' of English society. Taking his homosexual friend Richard Dawkins with him, he set off for a self-imposed exile in Italy, impractically choosing the city of Venice to settle in because of its 'myriad different kinds of light.' With the little money he had, he managed to pay for a modest hotel room and as a last extravagance hire the services of two young gondoliers and their craft, one of whom obligingly agreed to pose for more of Rolfe's nude photographs. In the manner of Lord Byron a century earlier, Rolfe set out to explore the Venetian canals. He relished the decaying atmosphere of the city that appeared to match his own melancholic temperament. His own money soon spent, he was compelled to rely on Dawkins's allowance and when his companion had the temerity to complain of Rolfe's extravagance he was met with a tirade of abuse. Within a month the disgruntled Dawkins had returned to England, leaving Rolfe to his own devices. To support himself he applied unsuccessfully for a job as a gondolier and then explored the possibility of setting up as a photographer but was unable to raise sufficient money to buy the necessary equipment.

Although his finances were depleted, his creative drive increased in intensity and the first two years in Venice saw Rolfe's most productive period as an author. As well as books, he constantly wrote letters to his supposed enemies in Britain including a vitriolic series attacking the *Daily Mail* newspaper and its proprietor Lord Northcliffe (1865–1922). On a lighter note, he began a homoerotic correspondence with Charles Masson Fox (1866–1935) in the hope of tempting him and his money to Venice. Fox belonged to the homosexual circle that included the Falmouth painter Henry Tuke and the writer John Gambril Nicholson (1866–1931). In England Fox had earned the respect of fellow homosexuals when he brought an action for blackmail against a woman who threatened she would reveal that he had seduced her son. Although Fox won his case, the bad publicity that resulted damaged his career. When Fox failed to take the bait, Rolfe desperately swallowed his pride and appealed to Richard Dawkins for help, promising to send him more nude photographs of Venetian boys. This correspondence was later taken as evidence that Rolfe was a persistent corrupter of children but these and other letters make it plain that he was interested only in youths in their late teens. When not composing these contentious letters, Rolfe began writing *Venetian Courtesy*, a series of stories of Venetian life featuring bronzed and youthful gondoliers.

Living from week to week on whatever credit he could raise, Rolfe placated his landlord at the Hotel Belle Vue with his old trick of pretending he was about to receive a large advance from his publisher in London. Finally, in April 1909, the landlord's patience ran out and Rolfe found himself where he had been so often before, out on the streets with barely more than the clothes he stood up in. For several nights he slept out in the gondola he still used until offered a week's lodging in an empty flat while the owners, an elderly clergyman and his wife, visited England. When they returned Rolfe refused their charitable offer to pay his fare back to England. In a curious way Rolfe's determination to remain in Venice in spite of the dangers to himself is reminiscent of the character of Gustav von Aschebach in Thomas Mann's *Death in Venice* whose love for a boy causes him to remain while deadly cholera stalks the city. Rolfe's fate too may have been sealed by the deprivation caused sleeping rough with little to eat during bitter cold weather. In April 1910 he became so ill that he collapsed and was taken to a local hospital suffering from pneumonia.

A month later Rolfe had sufficiently recovered to write optimistically 'I felt that my life has been handed back to me to have another try.' His luck also appeared to have turned when his old landlord at the Belle Bue agreed to take him back although he was given a dingy, rat-infested room at the back of the hotel. Yet the lack of interest in his work in London meant that even the modest advances of the past would no longer be forthcoming and when the landlord discovered the truth, Rolfe was once again thrown out of his lodgings. Homeless and in poor health he wandered the shores of the Lido looking for shelter. Then, remarkably, luck intervened in the form of a letter from London containing a cheque for £10 from

Queen Alexandra (1844–1925), the result of a begging letter he had written a few months earlier reminding the Queen that they had met when she had visited Venice. Then more letters arrived from England containing gifts of money. Rolfe was able to take a room in a more comfortable hotel and renovate his beloved gondola. The writer John Cowper Powys (1872–1963) on holiday in Venice that year recalled seeing him gliding past 'in a floating equipage that resembled the barge of Cleopatra ... in the stern, lying on a leopards skin was a personage who ... was one of the most whimsical writers and one of the most beguiling men of the great world'.

Throughout the summer of 1912 Rolfe seemed more at peace than he had been for years. He had acquired a companion, Thomas Wade-Brown, an ex-tea planter from Ceylon, who had become fascinated by Rolfe's writings and his quirky character. When their money ran out, the hotel owner found them a room a grand house overlooking the Grand Canal that was awaiting renovation. Rolfe used the last of his money to decorate the room with scarlet silk hangings although he failed to pay the poor seamstress for making the matching cushions and bedspread. That same year he completed his new novel, *The Desire and Pursuit of the Whole*, a strange tale of sexual ambiguity in which the hero rescues a boy from an earthquake and then discovering that he is really a girl takes her to Venice dressed as a boy gondolier.

The following year still in his scarlet room and still struggling to find the money to survive, Frederick Rolfe died quietly. On the morning of 25 October, Wade-Brown went into his bedroom to find his companion dead of a heart attack, his body still fully clothed and curiously with a loaded revolver in one of the pockets. Rolfe might well have composed his own obituary for in a passage in *The Desire and Pursuit of the Whole* he writes:

> *No fruit came from his sowing. Nothing was left in him, or of him, but an unconquerable capacity for endurance till sweet white Death should have leave to touch him, with an insuperable determination to keep his crisis from the hideous eyes of all men.*

Appropriately for such a disputatious man, even his grave became the subject of a quarrel, as the Venetian authorities were unwilling to grant him permanent burial until the bill was paid by his brother a decade later. Perhaps all that can be said of the Venetian exile of this most unusual man was that it was lived out in a place worthy of his exceptional gifts and singular character.

Later critics have said that Rolfe's problem as a writer was that he wrote the wrong books in the wrong place. Communicating with London publishers from Venice was never easy and the difficulties were exacerbated by Rolfe's prickly character. If his dealings with publishers were strained then his relations with his attempted literary collaborators were appalling. Rolfe claimed to like working with others but after the initial honeymoon period all these partnerships inevitably ended in failure. His behaviour towards them was later satirized in *The Unspeakable Skipton* by Pamela Hansford Johnson (1912–81). Rolfe's refusal to compromise on anything, least of all on his writing, also meant that his ornate and contrived prose style condemned him to a minority audience. A friend of 20 years, E. G. Hardy considered his life 'one of self-denying labour almost wholly unrewarded, which in almost every other profession could hardly have failed to win success.' In character he was uniquely ambiguous. His friend Canon Ragg said of him at the time of this death 'there was something definitely attractive about him as well as something repellent'.

After his death the myth of Baron Corvo began to grow following an article about him written by Sir Shane Leslie (1885–1971) in 1923. A decade later, the English writer A. J. A. Symons (1872–1963) published *The Quest for Corvo*, the first comprehensive study of the man, which proved so influential that it led to the founding of the Corvean Society. Symons's book opens with him being handed a copy of the then little known *Hadrian the Seventh*. After reading a few pages Symons was as captivated by the story as he was intrigued by its author. This discovery prompted him to search out a selection of Rolfe's letters in which he discovered that the writer of the fine and ornate prose of *Hadrian the Seventh* was also a cantankerous and self-centred sponger.

COMING OUT WITH JOHN ADDINGTON SYMONDS

There was no ambiguity, however, about the actions of John Addington (A. J.) Symonds. Once secure in his homosexuality, he became the most important figure in gay rights in 19th-century Britain and the first modern historian of same-sex love. Although bold and decisive in later life, his childhood bore an uncanny similarity to that of Edward Lear. Both were separated from their mothers as young boys and brought up in a predominantly female household. They were both also sickly children who bore the psychological scars of trauma into adult life. They also shared a tendency to depression, a tendency to fantasy and both sought exile to escape the stifling moral climate of Victorian England. Strangely for a man who was to promote openness in homosexual relationships, Symonds was appalled by what he witnessed at Harrow School where 'every boy of good looks had a female name, and was recognized either as a public prostitute or as some bigger fellow's "bitch"'. Symonds was even more scandalized when his friend, Alfred Pretor, told him that he was having an affair with the headmaster, Charles John Vaughan. Outraged more by the hypocrisy than the sexual activity, he became obsessed with seeing Vaughan brought to justice.

At the time Symonds was struggling with a growing awareness of his own homosexuality and the guilt and shame that he felt in himself, as he later admitted, was transferred to the authoritarian figure of the headmaster. When Symonds told his father the whole story, Symonds senior immediately wrote to Vaughan threatening to expose him unless he agreed to resign. Alfred Pretor was disgusted by what he saw as his friend's treachery and never spoke to him again, leaving Symonds with a lingering sense of guilt.

In 1859, when Symonds had moved on to Oxford University, he fell in love with Willie Dyer, a Bristol chorister three years his junior but managed to sublimate his emotions. Five years later Symonds was appointed a Fellow of Magdalen College and took a private pupil who wanted to gain entry to the college. The boy must have suspected his tutor's homosexual tendencies for when they fell out the boy attempted blackmail by alleging that Symonds 'had supported him in his pursuit of another chorister and that I shared his habits and was bent on the same path'. After an inquiry Symonds was officially cleared of any wrongdoing but was unable to prevent himself falling in love with another pupil about to go up to Oxford. This time the relationship was mildly physical and Symonds records in his diary that 'I stripped him naked and had sight, touch and mouth on these things.' To avoid further temptation, he took a short holiday to Italy and Switzerland until the passion cooled.

Life became increasingly complicated for A. J. Symonds for, in spite of his sexual orientation, he had succeeded, unlike Edward Lear, in making a conventional marriage and fathering four daughters. This was his most significant gesture in attempting to sublimate his homosexuality and to conform to a society where social and professional success depended upon appearing respectable and having an uneventful sex life.

The American writer Henry James (1843–1916) met Symonds in London and became fascinated by his predicament, which was not dissimilar to his own. James felt great sympathy for a man trapped in an unhappy marriage to a prim woman who detested his writing. Such a fate might well have befallen James himself had he remained in America and it inspired him to write a short story about a similarly unhappy couple.

Symonds's emotional problems were compounded by his reading Plato's *Dialogues* while at Oxford . They idealized male love although Benjamin Jowett's (1817–93) translation watered down the most specific sexual passages. This only caused confusion to men like Symonds who went through agonies in their search for an ideal but non-physical homosexual love.

By 1877, Symonds was a highly respected scholar with an extremely unhappy love life. His monumental work, *The Renaissance in Italy*, had begun to appear in print and he had narrowly missed being appointed Professor of Poetry at Oxford. Behind the conventional facade, Symonds was increasingly troubled by the homosexual impulses that he had managed to control. One February evening, after giving a lecture at the Royal Institution in London, he was taken by a friend to a male brothel near Regent's Park Barracks. What he experienced there was to completely change his life. He was introduced to a handsome 'brawny young soldier' with whom he eventually had sex. The sheer physicality of the encounter was a revelation to a man whose emotions had largely been confined to his work and he later recalled 'it was a lesson in sex as adventure, discovery and companionship as well as sensual pleasure'. This encounter convinced him that he must abandon the facade of heterosexuality. He told his wife the truth and assured her that their 'pure and faithful friendship' could continue. With little financial option but to continue the marriage and retain some vestige of respectability in late Victorian England his wife Catherine agreed.

Free of his past inhibitions, Symonds decided to travel in Europe where he could more openly express his homosexuality and be free of the conformist pressures of English society. It was his personal attempt to 'come out' and he chose a relative backwater of European society in which to do it. He had decided that his new life as a homosexual would begin in Switzerland and he went first to the quiet provincial city of Davos where he soon met the 19-year-old Christian Buol 'one of the finest specimens of robust, handsome, intelligent and gentle adolescence I have ever met with'. Abandoning the idea of travelling on to Egypt, Symonds decided to settle in Davos where he remained in exile for the rest of his life. Newly liberated of the moral constraints of England, he dedicated himself to freeing others. Speaking out for homosexuals became his mission and he began writing *A Problem in Greek Ethics*, the first modern defence of homosexuality in the English language. His purpose he said was 'to put the facts on record ... so that fellow-sufferers should feel that they are not alone'. The book was published in 1883 and it was followed a decade later by his *Memoirs*, the first overtly homosexual autobiography ever written. In this work he avoids the recently coined word 'homosexuality' in favour of such phrases as 'masculine love' or 'passion between males.' Unfortunately no London publisher was bold enough to take it on, so the *Memoirs* remained unpublished until 1984.

One of the most significant influences on the evolution of Symonds's ideas was the poetry of Walt Whitman. He became an immediate fan of the American poet's *Leaves of Grass* and particularly to a section known as the 'Calamus', in which Whitman describes the idealistic love of male comrades. To Symonds this seemed a modern interpretation of the same male love that was praised in Plato's *Symposium*. Symonds wanted to be seen as the British Whitman even though the American poet refused to acknowledge his own homosexuality. Whitman's positive and optimistic attitude to life greatly appealed to the Englishman who was fascinated by the possibility of gay men such as himself playing a far more positive role in the future of society. In 1874 he wrote to Walt Whitman thanking him for 'giving me a ground for the love of men ... for you have made men to be not ashamed of the noblest instinct of their nature. Women are beautiful; but to some, there is that which passes the love of women.' These sentiments were shared by Symonds's friend, the political philosopher Edward Carpenter (1844–1929), who was equally open about his homosexuality.

Carpenter also realized that Whitman's ideas were the modern expression of the Greek love of the distant past. Coming from a prosperous middle-class background like Symonds, Carpenter had in the 1870s at Cambridge followed the familiar pattern of being emotionally drawn to his fellow undergraduates. Carpenter also had a highly sensitive social conscience and felt an almost overwhelming sense of guilt at his family's wealth. In reading Walt Whitman, Carpenter managed to solve both problems by combining his socialism with his homosexuality. For a time he travelled in India, where he adopted many of the ideas contained in the local Hindu culture and its liberating emphasis on sexual activity. He also became an implacable opponent of colonialism and a champion of the young Mahatma Gandhi (1869–1948). In 1908 Edward Carpenter published a collection of essays that was one of the first readily available books in English to deal with homosexuality in a morally positive way. For decades it remained the crucial text in English that gave information, hope and support for homosexuals before the modern gay liberation movement came into existence.

In later life A. J. Symonds became a prolific correspondent, writing letters from Switzerland to other homosexuals including the poets Walt Whitman, Edmund Gosse (1849–1928), Charles Kains-Jackson (1857–1933), and Edward Carpenter (1844–1929). Together these letters make up a unique collection of recorded homosexual experiences at a time when social attitudes were changing but homophobic laws remained firmly in place. Symonds always wrote with a feverish energy as if making up for the time he had lost when living the life of a conventional Victorian family man. He completed his history of the Renaissance and went on to produce biographies of Shelley (1792–1822), Sir Philip Sidney (1554–86), Ben Jonson (1572–1637) and Michelangelo (1475–1564), whose nephew he condemned for changing the gender of offending love poems from male to female. As his fame spread within the English gay community, Symonds became a mentor figure among them because of his refusal to compromise over his sexuality or to keep a discreet silence. His house in Davos remained open for anyone who chose to call and avail themselves of his advice and experience.

From his deathbed in Rome in 1893, Symonds wrote to his wife Catherine asking her to give all his manuscripts, diaries, letters 'and other matters found in my books cupboard' to his friend Horatio Forbes Brown. He was insistent on this 'because I have written things you could not like to read, but which I have always felt justified and useful for society'. Symonds saw this testimony as his 'coming out' in the hope that this would help liberate others in a similar predicament. Catherine, however, having endured a lifetime of ignominy that she blamed on her husband's exile and his decision to live openly as a homosexual man, saw this as the final straw. She told Brown that she would not consent to having this material published and Brown had no alternative but to obey her wishes. Those readers who knew about Symonds's private life were bemused to find all references to his well-known homosexuality completely missing. The task of checking the proofs had been handed to his friend, Edmund Gosse, who had proceeded to emasculate them further. Even more astonishingly, when Brown died in 1926, he left Symonds's memoirs and papers, including Symonds's sexual diary and his correspondence with fellow homosexuals, to Gosse. In an act of literary vandalism, Gosse took all the papers out into his garden and burned the lot, claiming later that he had done so to preserve Symonds's good name. In fact, he had done it to protect his own, for some of the letters must have been to Gosse himself. Fearful of being 'outed' as a homosexual, he had thus betrayed everything that Symonds stood for. All that remained was Symonds's *Memoirs*, a work fittingly inspired by Benvenuto Cellini's own forthright *Vita*.

THE TRAGEDY OF OSCAR WILDE

In the last decades of the 19th century, while Italy retained its attraction for homosexuals and lesbians, it was Paris that became the new magnet for exiles. The liberal laws on sexuality introduced in the *Code Napoléon* are part of the explanation together with the flowering of French culture in all the arts. So, it was here that Irish writer Oscar Wilde went after his release from prison in 1897, characteristically preferring the flamboyant French metropolis in which to display his now proven homosexuality rather than A. J. Symonds's far more discreet retreat in Switzerland.

Wilde was in a poor state of health when he arrived in the city after his two years of hard labour. A career that had begun with such promise appeared to have ended in public ridicule and contempt. Only after Wilde's death did his reputation rise phoenix-like from the ashes until he was once more recognized as the greatest comic dramatist of the 19th century. Today, those who brought him down are universally reviled and their names are generally forgotten. However, when Wilde was a young man the contest between the moral majority and the aesthetic minority was at its height. One of the chief protagonists of the latter was the writer and critic Walter Pater (1839–94), who Wilde first met when he arrived at Magdalen College, Oxford, in 1874.

Wilde was captivated by Pater's aesthetic concept of 'art for art's sake' – the belief that beauty needed no other justification than itself. For conventional moralists, however, Pater's aestheticism was little more than a euphemism for homosexuality. The blunt, no-nonsense world of late Victorian morality and commerce had little time for Pater, or his precious ideas. The rumours of homosexuality at the University of Oxford where Pater taught seemed to confirm the dangers of aestheticism. His fellow critic and self-declared protector of public morals, W. T. Courthope, announced in 1876 that 'we repudiate the effeminate desires which Mr. Pater, the mouthpiece of our artistic "culture", would encourage in society.' Any doubts that Pater and his friends were leading England's young men astray appeared to be confirmed when it was revealed that the great aesthete had been involved in homosexual relationships with the painter Simeon Solomon (1840–1905) and the poet Algernon Charles Swinburne (1837–1909). Solomon was jailed for 'gross indecency' and was as shunned by society as Lord Byron had been. Had Oscar Wilde taken more notice of Solomon's fate, he might well have avoided his own downfall.

The moral climate of Britain was changing and the *Criminal Law Amendment Act* of 1885 marked the triumph of the various pressure groups that had been campaigning against what they saw as the moral degeneration of the country. The Act was originally designed to provide more protection to vulnerable women and girls and its provisions included the suppression of brothels. However, during its unopposed second reading, an amendment was introduced by a radical Member of Parliament, Henry Labouchere (1831–1912), suggesting that control of homosexuality be included in its provisions. The House agreed and when the bill was finally passed all homosexual acts, whether in private or in public, and not just sodomy, became a legal offence. This retrograde action left Britain as one of the few European countries in which even mutual masturbation by adult men in the privacy of their own homes was illegal. France, for example, had decriminalized all homosexual acts between consenting adults almost a century earlier. It was now a dangerous time for individuals such as Oscar Wilde who could clearly be recognized as an aesthete and who went about Oxford and later London clad in flamboyant dress. With his velvet coat edged with braid, knee-breeches and black silk stockings, soft loose shirt with a wide floppy collar, lavender gloves and green carnation he provoked the ire of the respectable classes.

At first protected by his undoubted talent as a dramatist, Oscar Wilde ignored the hostility and became the sexual protégé of the

Canadian-born journalist Robert Ross (1869–1918), allegedly his first male lover. In what should have proved a warning to Wilde, Ross had been accused of having sex with two boys, aged 14 and 15, a few years before Wilde's imprisonment. The boys confessed to their parents but because they, too, could have gone to prison along with their seducer, the parents decided not to go to the police. With Ross's encouragement, Wilde also began to look for young boys and seek out male prostitutes. Although Wilde talked about romantic love for 'fair, slim choirboys', he soon settled for more readily available rough-trade lads. Most of these risky encounters took place in gay bars or brothels and Wilde revelled in the danger as much as in the sexual pleasure, describing it as 'feasting with panthers'.

Wilde's self-destructive behaviour has been attributed to many causes, among them the fact that he came from a dysfunctional family. His father was a heavy drinker and a philanderer who already supported three illegitimate children before his marriage. Both parents were obsessed, like Oscar himself, with appearance, indicating insecurity and a fear of abandonment. Oscar's own heavy drinking also suggested an addictive personality. Decades after Wilde's death, one of his greatest admirers, the poet W. H. Auden (1907–73), offered a different explanation, writing that he thought most of Wilde's problems resulted from his being overindulged by his mother, which had produced feelings of unworthiness that is characteristic of addicts. Others have suggested that Wilde had an unusual addiction to romance and was incapable of really caring about the other person involved. To someone such as Wilde the thrill of a relationship would come not from the sex or the companionship but from an illusion of love itself.

With such a potentially dangerous inheritance it was probably only a matter of time before Oscar Wilde ran into serious trouble. A clear warning that public opinion was far less tolerant than he supposed came after the publication of his homoerotic novel *The Picture of Dorian Gray* in 1890. A personally offensive and malicious attack on Wilde appeared in the *St James Gazette* written by a self-appointed defender of public morals, Samuel Henry Jeye. In response, Wilde wrote to the editor defending his work and loftily dismissing Jeye's pseudo-ethical criticism in dealing with artistic work. He then added insult to injury by arrogantly including Jeye's and other hostile reviews, quoted verbatim, to the next printed edition of the novel. Wilde summed up the whole furore with the words 'there is no such thing as a moral or an immoral book. Books are well written, or badly written. That is all.' For the time being, Wilde's was the last word but he had made enemies in the press and they would now be watching for him to make a mistake.

Wilde's affections now focused on one man, Lord Alfred Douglas (1870–1945), the son of a sporting homophobe, the Marquess of Queensberry. Lord Alfred, better known as Bosie, was openly gay, a spendthrift, gambler and a dropout from Oxford who routinely sponged off Wilde. A less disingenuous man than Wilde would have seen that the relationship would inevitably threaten the success he had began to enjoy as the eminent author of *The Importance of Being Earnest*. Lord Queensberry, who spent much of his time among the sporting fraternity, was particularly sensitive to sexual matters having personal problems of his own. His second wife had won an annulment soon after their marriage because of the 'malformation of the parts of generation, frigidity and impotence'. On 18 February, 1895, after two earlier skirmishes when he had burst into Wilde's house in Mayfair and threatened him with violence, Queensberry left his calling card at the Albermarle Club famously addressed to Oscar Wilde 'posing as a somdomite' [sic]. Wilde, relying too heavily on his celebrity as his defence, brought a complaint of criminal libel against the Marquess, who was arrested but later freed on bail. Returning from a holiday in Europe and unaware of the danger he was in, Wilde was met on his arrival by family and friends urging him to drop the charges. They pointed out that if he should lose the case, the Crown would then have no choice but to charge him with gross indecency under the *Criminal Law Amendment Act*. 'Who are you to set back the clock 50 years?' his friend, the writer Frank Harris (1856–1931), was supposed to have asked. 'You haven't a dog's chance.'

Given the Marquess of Queensberry's financial resources it was not difficult for him to hire private detectives to investigate the homosexual demi-monde that Wilde frequented and the salacious details of Wilde's private life were soon leaked to the press. A day or two before the trial, Wilde was appalled to learn that the defence had come up with the names of 10 boys he had solicited, together with some incriminating letters that he had written to them.

At the very start of the proceedings, Wilde was humiliatingly shown to be a liar for when asked his age he gave it as 39. Calmly the defence council, Sir Edward Carson, produced a document showing that he was in fact 40 years old. After this bad start, Wilde committed the cardinal sin of any witness under cross-examination by profering more information than had been asked for. When questioned about one particular boy he volunteered the information 'it is not true that I met him by appointment one evening and took him on the road to Lancing, kissing him and indulging in familiarities on the way.' It became clear that Wilde's libel action was doomed but his own counsel, Sir Edward Clarke, offered him a compromise with Queensberry. In return for the charge of libel being withdrawn, the Marquess might agree to abandon any further action and no criminal charges would be brought against Wilde. However, neither Carson nor Queensberry would relent; the latter was determined to see Wilde totally destroyed.

As soon as the libel action ended, Queensberry ordered his solicitor to send the notes from the libel trial and all the accumulated evidence to Scotland Yard. The authorities had little choice but to arrest Wilde on charges of gross indecency. Queensberry gloatingly informed Wilde of what he had done ending his note with the threat 'I will not prevent your flight, but if you take my son with you, I will shoot you like a dog.' Again Wilde hesitated, torn between standing his ground and fleeing into exile, uncertain if he would ever return to England again. His wife Constance, who had stood by him until now, urged him to go, as did the majority of his friends. Yet Wilde displayed his own version of Spartan courage and decided that the prospect of prison was preferable to suffering the ignominy and disgrace of being seen to run away.

Wilde's greatest misfortune was in facing a prosecution for 'acts of gross indecency with other male persons' so soon after the Cleveland Street scandal of 1889.

This incident began when the police discovered a group of young telegraph boys making extra money by working in a male brothel frequented by some members of the aristocracy. One of the most frequent clients was Lord Arthur Somerset (1851–1926), an equerry to the Prince of Wales. Somerset, together with the brothel keeper Charles Hammond, managed to flee abroad before a prosecution could be brought against them but the event confirmed a growing public perception of an upper-class decadence that was corrupting working-class youth. Wilde had prophetically alluded to the scandal in *The Picture of Dorian Gray* published the year after. Armed with the provisions of the new *Criminal Law Amendment Act*, the police prepared their case but pressure from the Lord Chancellor ensured that Somerset and other high-class customers escaped prosecution. Wilde, however, had no such protection and his scandalous reputation made it certain that the case against him would proceed.

On April 26, the trial of Oscar Wilde began with both Bosie and Robbie Ross having slipped safely out of the country. The charges Wilde faced were gross indecency, conspiracy to commit gross indecency and sodomy. The prosecutor, Charles Gill, by chance an old acquaintance of Wilde's at Oxford, called a succession of young men to the witness box, some ordinary working-class boys, others part-time male prostitutes.

In spite of the peril he was in, Wilde maintained the eloquence for which he had become famous. When asked to explain a sentence he had written about 'the love that dare not speak its name', Wilde delivered a moving definition of Greek love as:

> *The great affection of an elder for a younger man as there was between David and Jonathan, such as Plato made the very basis of his philosophy, and such as you find in the sonnets of Michelangelo and Shakespeare. It is that deep, spiritual affection that is as pure as it is perfect ... It is in this century misunderstood, so much misunderstood that it may be described as 'the Love that dare not speak its name', and on account of it I am placed where I am now. It is beautiful,*

it is fine, it is the noblest form of affection. There is nothing unnatural about it, and it repeatedly exists between an elder and a younger man, when the elder has intellect, and the younger man has all the joy, hope and glamour of life before him. That it should be so, the world does not understand. The world mocks at it and sometimes puts one in the pillory for it.

It was a powerful justification for his feeling if not his actions and the jury were unable to reach a verdict, meaning that the case went for retrial.

A month later Wilde returned to court a second time, with Alfred Taylor, to face the same charges. Wilde again denied his proclivities but the confessions of many of his partners assured his conviction. The presiding judge, Justice Wills, was a confirmed homophobe who considered sodomy only slightly less heinous than murder. In summing up, he paid particular attention to the letters between Wilde and Bosie, and announced that this had been the worst case of homosexual depravity he had come across. After only two hours of deliberation, the jury returned a unanimous verdict of guilty on all counts except one. Justice Wills addressed the defendants with words of the utmost gravity:

Oscar Wilde and Alfred Taylor, the crime of which you have been convicted is so bad that one has to put stern restraint upon one's self to prevent one's self from describing, in language which I would rather not use, the sentiments which must rise to the breast of every man of honour who has heard the details of these two terrible trials.

He then passed sentence, stating that it was the severest that the law allowed but that in 'my judgement it is totally inadequate for such a case as this. The sentence of the Court is that each of you be imprisoned and kept to hard labour for two years.' At this Wilde was seen to visibly stagger and appealed to be heard with the words 'My God. May I say nothing, My Lord?', but Wills merely waved his hand at the jailers, gathered his papers and walked out as the prisoners were led away.

At the time, Wilde had two plays playing to packed houses in the West End of London but professional disaster soon followed personal disgrace. The American tour of *A Woman of No Importance* was cancelled and the sale of his new play *Salomé* fell through. As with Lord Byron and William Beckford, many of his old friends now abandoned him and Wilde became a pariah. Those who did stand by him were ostracized by London society and some were evicted from their apartments or expelled from clubs.

In a final coup de grâce, the Marquess of Queensberry obtained a judgement against Wilde for the £600 he had spent defending himself against the libel charges plus the court costs. He demanded immediate payment in full, forcing Wilde into almost immediate bankruptcy. Some of his most prized possessions including the first editions of his own plays and paintings by his friends, Whistler (1834–1903) and Aubrey Beardsley (1872–1898), were seized by bailiffs and sold at auction to pay the costs. By then Wilde's marriage had fallen apart and his sons were taken from him. Perhaps for Wilde the most humiliating experience of all was to see his plays taken off the London stage. Worse was to come, however, for while standing on Clapham Station handcuffed to two warders en route for Reading Gaol, a man came up and spat in his face. For the rest of his life he wept whenever he recalled his utter degradation at that moment.

For a man mocked for lack of moral fibre, Wilde faced the prospect of imprisonment with unexpected stoicism. Soon after his arrival at Reading, the prison chaplain thought him willing to face his punishment without flinching but as soon as he 'had to encounter the daily routine of prison life his fortitude began to give way and rapidly collapsed altogether. He is now quite crushed and broken ... in fact some of our most experienced officers openly say that they don't think he will be able to go through the two years.' Yet he did survive in spite of the daily degradation. As the days passed, he began to consider where he should live after release and the prospect of moving to a new life in France became appealing.

He had received sympathy from many French newspapers and while he was still in jail his new play *Salomé* had been staged in Paris to great acclaim. He wrote poignantly to the producers of his gratitude 'that at this time of disgrace and shame I should still be regarded as an artist'.

Disgraced and humiliated by his incarceration, Wilde departed from England on 20 May 1897 and was met at Dieppe by Robbie Ross. This most faithful of friends had booked him into Hotel Sandwich under the pseudonym, Sebastian Melmoth, and filled his room with books and flowers. Of more practical help in those first days of exile was the £800 that Ross had collected in England from sympathizers. Having endured the privations of jail, Wilde began frittering the money away on luxuries until given a stern warning by Ross that he must now live more frugally. This did not stop him throwing a number of boisterous dinner parties in local restaurants. Alarmed by the commotion caused by their celebrated if infamous visitor, the Dieppe authorities warned that he must behave more discreetly.

The locals generally ignored him and his only really painful experiences were to be avoided by Aubrey Beardsley and cut dead in the street by the painter Jacques-Emile Blanche (1861–1942) – experiences that recalled the humiliation suffered by Lord Byron at the hands of his erstwhile friends. Wilde decided to move to the nearby village of Berneval-sur-Mer, where he took rooms at the Hotel de la Plage. There he received his young friend, the writer André Gide, who found Wilde much coarsened in appearance by prison but strangely spiritually enlightened by the experience. Gide thought his host's natural selfishness had been tempered by pity having witnessed the misery of children imprisoned for minor offences. He had also been deeply moved by the kindness of some of his fellow inmates who displayed real concern for him and one man in particular who took the blame when they were both discovered talking in the yard.

Wilde's exile did not appear to have embittered him against the English either. When Queen Victoria's (1819–1901; Queen of United Kingdom of Great Britain and Ireland 1837–1901) Diamond

Jubilee was celebrated that June, Wilde had the main function room of the hotel decorated with Union Jacks and bunting for a party with his new friends – the priest, the postman, the local schoolmaster and 15 of his pupils. He moved into a rented house and began composing 'The Ballad of Reading Gaol'. Fatally, he also wrote to Lord Alfred Douglas asking him to come back as 'I feel that my only hope of again doing beautiful work is being with you.' This attempt at a rapprochement with Bosie proved the final straw for his wife, Constance, who broke off all contact with him.

Two months later, restored enough in spirits to move to Paris, Wilde set off for the city hoping to meet up with Bosie and travel on with him to Italy. On arrival he encountered an Irish–American writer he knew, Vincent O'Sullivan (1868–1940), and invited him to lunch. After they had eaten, he admitted to O'Sullivan that he had neither the money to pay for the meal nor to buy his train ticket to Italy. Relaxed and mellowed by the wine, O'Sullivan generously offered to provide both and even drove Wilde to the station. At Aix-les-Bains he met Bosie before continuing on to Posilipo near Naples from where he informed Constance, who was staying at Genoa, that although he was with Bosie he would still like to visit her. She replied with an unambiguously angry letter and cancelled the modest allowance she had been providing for him. Short of money, their financial plight was made worse by Lady Queensberry informing her son that if he remained with Wilde she would cut off his own generous allowance. She even wrote to Wilde offering him a paltry £200 if he would agree not to see her son again. Once he would have disdainfully dismissed her offer but now, desperate for money, he meekly accepted. Bosie went on alone to Rome while his erstwhile lover had little choice but to return to Paris.

Reduced to taking scruffy lodgings at the Hotel de Nice on the Left Bank, Wilde sank into depression until excellent reviews of 'The Ballad of Reading Gaol' arrived from England. Copies of the poem had been sent privately as a gesture of gratitude to those friends that had stood by him. Among them was André Gide, who encountered Wilde a few weeks later sitting outside the Café de la Paix. Gide was shocked by the marked deterioration in his friend's appearance in just a year. Sitting opposite Wilde, he noted that his hat had lost its shine and his shirt collar and cuffs were frayed and dirty. They talked for a while then as Gide rose to go, Wilde took his arm and whispered sadly 'I think you ought to know that I have absolutely nothing to live on.' Others visiting Paris who had known him at the height of his powers also found Wilde a pathetic figure. When Constance died without seeing him again, he inherited her small legacy but it was not enough to fund his drinking nor his appetite for young boys. Bosie always maintained that it was at this time that Robbie Ross had 'dragged him back to homosexual practices' during the summer of 1897, which they spent together in Berneval. In a letter to Ross, Wilde later lamented 'Today I bade good-bye, with tears and one kiss, to the beautiful Greek boy ... he is the nicest boy you ever introduced to me.'

With nothing more to lose, Wilde abandoned all discretion and 'came out' openly, abandoning all mention of Greek love in favour of giving his friends down-to-earth descriptions of his brief sexual encounters. He had begun seeing Bosie again, although the physical relationship between them had gone forever. They now had even less money as Bosie's inveterate gambling consumed almost his entire income leaving them little for food or entertaining. To economize, Wilde moved into cheaper accommodation at the Hotel d'Alsace, where he was said to have made his famous comment that either he or the wallpaper must go. Reluctant to leave Paris, Wilde was persuaded by the writer Frank Harris to visit him at Cannes the following summer, where he became friendly with a young fisherman. Back in Paris he found himself unable to write anything new and was further dispirited when the English newspaper ignored the published version of *The Importance of Being Earnest*. Now losing his teeth and unable to afford false ones, he made such an unprepossessing sight when he met the soprano Dame Nellie Melba (1861–1931) in the street that she opened her handbag and gave him all the money in it.

In the spring of 1900, another benefactor paid for him to visit Italy for what would be the last time. At Nice, in the South of France, he told a friend that he had once known three lads who lived in the town who were like bronze statues, quite perfect in form. Then he added with a touch of his characteristic wit that 'English lads are chryselephantine. Swiss people are carved out of wood with a rough knife, most of them; the others are carved out of turnips.' Arriving in Rome, Wilde joined a queue waiting for an audience with the Pope and was taken on an escorted tour of the city by, as he claimed, a particularly handsome young guide. Reluctantly he returned to Paris, where his health began to seriously deteriorate. His face covered in what might well have been the red blotches of tertiary syphilis, Wilde now spent most of his time in bed. Worst of all his ailments was an excruciatingly painful abscess in one ear that had to be later operated on in his hotel room, as he was unable to move. The treatment brought little relief and the pain continued unabated, only being relieved by increasingly large doses of morphine. On 29 November, Robbie Ross arrived to find his friend near death and summoned a Catholic priest to baptise Wilde and give him the Last Rites. This was the procedure that had been agreed between them years earlier. Early the next morning Oscar Wilde died and Ross arranged for the body to be laid out in a clean nightshirt and for a last photograph to be taken. There were just 14 mourners at the funeral and as the prayers ended Bosie was seen to stagger and almost fall into the grave himself.

Oscar Wilde was perhaps the first gay victim of modern celebrity culture. 'If you wish for reputation and fame in the world,' he had once ironically advised, 'take every opportunity of advertising yourself.'

His miserable exile and squalid end was the price that he paid for outraging the conventional morality of his time but the very openness of his behaviour together with his undoubted genius as a great dramatist would earn him a rare and unusual immortality. Today Oscar Wilde's tombstone in the Père Lachaise cemetery in Paris is a place of pilgrimage and bears over 1,000 lipstick kisses – a small atonement by society for having driven such an original and talented man into undeserved exile and an early grave.

HENRY JAMES AND E. M. FORSTER – ATTITUDES TO EXILE

The fate of Oscar Wilde provided an awful warning to many of his gay contemporaries about the dangers of openly 'coming out' in a society governed by sexual intolerance. While Oscar Wilde had flaunted his homosexuality, the American novelist Henry James carefully hid his own and refused to sign a petition calling for Wilde's release from prison. Although driven by homosexual desires, James was adamant that he would reveal little of himself other than in his novels. This wariness was tested early in 1895 when James was asked by Mrs Daniel Sargent Curtis, an American expatriate hostess, to write an appreciation of A. J. Symonds, two years after his death. Unaware of James's sexual orientation and believing that a shared love of Italy was sufficient inducement, Mrs Curtis was shocked and mystified when James wanted nothing to do with the project. Perhaps James recalled writing to Symonds to tell him that they were both 'victims of a common passion'. He was never to repeat such openness again nor deviate from his policy of complete silence on sexual matters.

James grew up in an American society that had a long history of hostility to homosexuality. As early as 1610, while still struggling to survive, the Virginia Colony brought in a law proscribing the death penalty for sodomy, a lead that was followed by Massachusetts 31 years later. These Puritan settlers even took action against lesbians when such relationships were largely being ignored in Europe. In 1649 two women were punished at Plymouth for 'lewd offences ... committed on a bed'. It was not until 1682 that the Quaker colony of Pennsylvania abolished the death penalty for sodomy and another century would pass before Thomas Jefferson (1743–1826) persuaded the government of Virginia to substitute castration for execution.

In his own youth Henry James had witnessed the hostile reception that Walt Whitman's *Leaves of Grass* provoked, when published in 1855. Many thought its references to male love pornographic and obscene. One critic asserted that Whitman was guilty of 'that horrible sin not to be mentioned among Christians'. As a result of the controversy the State Department fired him from his civil service job and attempted to ban the book. Some publishers refused to accept later editions of the work and Whitman even agreed to remove the offending passages to placate them. The lesson for James was that being open about one's sexual orientation in 19th-century American society was tantamount to social ruin. The transparency of Whitman's emotions were clear in his work. After Oscar Wilde met the poet in America in 1882, he wrote to the homosexual rights activist George Cecil Ives (1867–1950) that there was no doubt about the poet's sexual orientation for 'I have the kiss of Walt Whitman still on my lips.' In 1890, A. J. Symonds asked Whitman directly if comradeship with other men, the emotional heart of Whitman's poems, depended upon a physical relationship, only to receive a blunt denial. Grown wary after years of suspicion and hostility towards him, Whitman replied defensively that he had six illegitimate children of his own and resented any inference that he might not be a full-blooded heterosexual. None of these supposed children were ever traced and Whitman's claim towards the end of his life, that he had enjoyed dozens of affairs with women was simply an attempt to counter the suggestion that appeared in the *New York Herald* suggesting that he had never had a relationship with a woman.

As a writer Whitman was not alone in attracting the wrath of the American morality lobby. The poet Fitz-Greene Halleck (1790–1867) had come under similar attack a generation earlier when he betrayed signs of gay sympathies in his own work. Halleck became known as 'the American Byron' and shared the English poet's same contempt for cant. The puritanical hypocrisy of American society appalled him – while it preached conformism and respectability it condoned the cruel treatment of slaves, native American Indians and the subjugation of women. While serving in the army in the war of 1812 against the British, Halleck fell in love with a young doctor named Joseph Rodman Drake and together they produced a highly successful series of satirical odes known as the 'Croaker' poems. By 1827, Halleck was as famous in America as Lord Byron had been in England but would suffer a similar fall from public grace. After Drake died of consumption at the age of 25, the press launched a vitriolic attack on Halleck suggesting that his verse was morally unhealthy because of its homosexual undertones. Halleck might have been hounded out of the country had he not made the decision to avoid future controversy and to keep a low profile. Consequently, his work suffered as he bowed to bland moral conformism.

The hostility that greeted Whitman and Halleck's mild attempts to portray same-sex love was still apparent in American society when Henry James was growing up in a wealthy New York family. From the first, James felt that he had to compete against his brilliant brother William, who later became one of the leading philosophers of his day. This sibling rivalry, his problematic sexuality and a growing desire to become a great writer directed him towards a lifelong exile in Europe. Fortunately his peripatetic father had taken his children with him on frequent business trips to Europe where they remained long enough to attend local schools. However, these enlightening visits ended with the outbreak of the American Civil War in 1861 and the James family became confined to Cambridge, Massachusetts. It was at this time that the 18-year-old James sustained an injury while helping to put out a fire in nearby Newport. This 'obscure hurt', as he later referred to it, altered his life forever. This 'extraordinarily intimate' injury later became a fascination for James's biographers who speculated that he had damaged his testicles, which led to the loss of his sexual drive and explained his lack of physical interest in women. Given James's secretive persona, this injury story might well have provided him with a very convenient explanation and a cover for his real interest – handsome young men.

Bored by life in Massachusetts, James sailed for Europe in October 1875. Although he eventually established a home in England, his first destination was Paris. There, he enthusiastically sought out the intellectual coterie that had made the French novel supreme in mid 19th-century literature. First he paid court to the great novelist Gustav Flaubert (1821–80) and through his circle soon met every important person in the French literary world. The move to Paris seemed to liberate him both creatively and emotionally for he fell in love with Paul Zhukovsky there. This young Russian aristocrat was obsessed by the music of Richard Wagner and later became the German's favourite set designer. While maintaining his customary wariness when dealing with emotional matters, James's letters to Zhukovsky make clear his deep attachment to him up until a troubling event occurred in the summer of 1880.

James had accepted Zhukovsky's invitation to join him at Posilippo near Naples where, to his dismay, James found his previously refined and aesthetic host surrounded by an 'immoral group' of young men, who made no secret of their gayness. James was horrified by their overt behaviour and sensed that it would be dangerous to associate himself too closely with such companions. After just three days James left Posilippo and went to Sorrento alone. His swift departure might also have been caused by sexual jealousy because it was obvious that Zhukovsky was conducting an openly homosexual liaison with one of the group, a young Neapolitan named Peppino. Instead of removing James's inhibitions about his feelings for other men, the incident only served to make him more cautious and reserved. From that moment, James remained firmly in the closet and any mention that he might take a physical interest in other men would send him into a panic. The novelist Hugh Walpole, a prominent member of the London gay literary set, along with Noel Coward (1899–1973), Ivor Novello (1893–1951), W. H. Auden (1907–73) and Christopher Isherwood (1904–86), claimed to have once propositioned the elderly James, who flew into a blind panic and kept repeating, to Walpole's amusement 'I can't! I can't!'

This fear of discovery affected everything that James did and explains his refusal in 1895 of Mrs Curtis's request to write the short biography of A. J. Symonds. Mrs Curtis's invitation, with its innocent implication that Symonds and James had been friends, deeply alarmed the latter and he sought desperately for an excuse to reject the project. Finally, he produced a face-saving formula, saying that he had been aware of Symonds's 'strangely morbid and hysterical nature', in other words his overt gayness, and he could not write about him without referring to it. This according to James would have to be 'an affectation; and yet to deal with it either ironically or explicitly would be a Problem, a problem beyond me.'

James's decision to forgo marriage and to suppress his sexuality confined him to a lonely, solitary life, although it did enable him to channel all his energy into his work. Much of this ambiguity is apparent in his writing where it colours his portrayal of male friendships. Critics have noticed that as his career progressed, his work becomes increasingly descriptive of male relationships. In his 1903 novella, *The Beast in the Jungle*, James tells the story of a man who spends his life convinced that some 'rare and strange, possibly prodigious and terrible' destiny awaits him, only to realize that in waiting for this event he has missed out on what life really had to offer.

James's fellow writer E. M. Forster (1879–1970), rather than going permanently into exile, reserved much of his gay activity for visits to Egypt or India. Even in England, Forster's relationships were not with members of his own class but with visiting Indians. Having, like James, witnessed the downfall of Oscar Wilde, Forster was acutely aware of what could happen to any public figure who revealed his homosexuality. Such unfair persecution inspired Forster's anger at this and other social and political injustices. When in his 80s he noted bitterly in his diary 'how annoyed I am with Society for wasting my time by making homosexuality criminal. The subterfuges, the self-consciousness that might have been avoided.' In the repressive society in which Forster grew up, it was not surprising that he trod the thin line between secrecy and openness in his sexual behaviour. His homosexuality manifested itself in an erotic preference for Arabs and Indians and for men of the lower social classes. He believed such people had a natural vitality that his own esoteric world of scholarship and refinement lacked. This led him to romanticize the working classes and to attack the injustices of the class system at home and British imperialism abroad.

The openness of Forster's character can be seen in his close association with the Bloomsbury Group of intellectuals that included the economist John Maynard Keynes (1883–1946), the novelist Virginia Woolf (1882–1941) and the artists Vanessa Bell (1879–1961; Woolf's sister) and Duncan Grant (1885–1978). Highly creative as individuals, they shared a hostility to materialistic realism in painting and literature but reserved much of their anger for society's repression of sexual equality. Their ambition was to establish a new social order based upon liberation from conventional behaviour and to make love more important than monogamy. This desire for sexual freedom was enthusiastically practised by the Bloomsbury Group members, who became involved in complicated sexual relationships with one other. In 1925, Virginia Woolf began a passionate affair with Vita Sackville-West (1892–1962), which inspired her novel *Orlando*, a classic of gay fiction that argues love and passion are irrelevant to gender.

This was certainly true of another member of the group, the writer Lytton Strachey (1880–1932) who, although predominantly homosexual, proposed first to Virginia Stephen (Woolf's maiden name before her marriage to Leo Woolf) and then shared a platonic marriage with the Surrealist painter Dora Carrington (1893–1932) until they both fell in love with the same man. Carrington promptly married him and all three set up house together. The cross-dressing Carrington also had affairs with women, once telling a friend that she had enjoyed 'more ecstasy with female lovers than with men and suffered no shame.' This kind of behaviour was typical of the Bloomsbury set, a group whose members were committed to a rejection of what they felt were the strictures and taboos of Victorianism on religious, artistic, social, and sexual matters. They remained a fairly tight-knit group for many years; recent biographers have detailed their tangled personal relations. By the 1920s Bloomsbury's reputation as a cultural circle was fully established to the extent that its mannerisms were parodied and Bloomsbury became a widely used term for an insular, snobbish aestheticism, verging on the effete. To the wider public it became synonymous with elitism and at the start of the First World War (1914–18) was associated with a deeply unpatriotic and unpopular pacifism.

Given his association with this heady world of free loving intellectuals it may seem strange that after an early flirtation at

Cambridge, Forster did not experience a full gay relationship of any duration until he was aged nearly 40. His sexual frustration during this period is reflected in his work and troubled him almost as much as his homosexuality itself. In 1907, when he was 26, Forster was living an emotionally unsatisfying life as an only child caring for his ailing mother in Surrey and complaining to friends that he was 'leading the life of a little girl tied to home'. Then into his life came the 17-year-old, future Sir Syed Ross Masood (1889–1937), who would become an eminent Indian Muslim educationalist in later life.

Tall, handsome and aristocratic in bearing, Masood was the great love of Forster's life and the inspiration for his most celebrated novel, *A Passage to India*. It has been suggested that protagonist Adela Quested's attraction in the novel to Dr Aziz, the Indian character, a strictly taboo relationship for a British memsahib, echoes Forster's own repressed desire for Masood. Local reaction to this exotic newcomer who had come to Forster for tuition in preparation for Oxford was predictably hostile. However, Masood's proud self-assurance made him immune to petty racism. Occasionally, Forster recalls, when Masood became bored with the Latin lessons he would pick his slightly built tutor up in his arms and tickle him until he burst out laughing. Their intimacy continued throughout Masood's undergraduate years at Oxford, when they wrote to each other almost every day. Suddenly Masood's letters become more formal suggesting that something had occurred between them. Perhaps Forster had transgressed by confessing the sexual nature of his love and Masood felt unable to respond. Forster later wrote 'I wish very much he had felt, if only once, what I felt for him for I should have no sense of wasted time.' However, the cordiality returned once Forster accepted the role of loving a younger man from a distance in a relationship that would never achieve a physical reality. They became each other's confidante, Masood telling Forster of his troubled marriage and Forster recounting his rare homosexual encounters. These included a period when the pacifist Forster refused to fight in the First World War (1914–18) and went to work for the Red Cross in Alexandria, where he lived with an Egyptian tram conductor,

Mohammed el Adl. When Masood returned to India, Forster visited him for six months.

When Forster returned to England, he became literary editor of the left-wing *Daily Herald* but the lure of the East remained and in 1921 he left for India to take up the post of personal secretary to the Maharaja of Dewas.

Many homosexuals have attacked Forster for failing to have the courage to 'come out' in English society, but given the conservatism of the period in which he lived, his reticence is understandable. The criticism of Forster that is perhaps more justified is based on his decision not to have his novel *Maurice* published during his lifetime. This homosexual love story did not appear in print until 1971 and was controversial even then. It proved to those outside his immediate circle that E. M. Forster was indeed a homosexual.

Forster claimed that the inspiration for his book was the relationship between his friends, Edward Carpenter and George Merrill. Once when visiting them at their house in Surrey, Forster experienced his only physical contact with Merrill:

> *He touched my backside – gently and just above the buttocks. I believe he touched most people's. The sensation was unusual and I still remember it, as I remember the position of a long vanished tooth. He made a profound impression on me and touched a creative spring.*

Forster was to make an equally profound impression on the writer Christopher Isherwood, who visited him in 1932 after reading the manuscript of *Maurice*. Isherwood was moved to be in the presence of:

> *... this great prophet of their tribe who declares that there can be real love, love without limits or excuse, between two men. Here he is, humble in his greatness, unsure of his own genius.*

Touched by Isherwood's praise for his book, Forster leant forward and gently kissed him on the cheek.

AMERICAN LESBIANS IN PARIS

While throughout the 18th and early 19th centuries, Italy continued to be the place of choice for some exiled homosexuals from northern Europe and America, others had begun choosing Paris as their base.

Although the city had suffered greatly from the siege ending the Franco–Prussian War (1870–71) and the subsequent Commune of Paris uprising of 1871, it had recovered rapidly to become the artistic capital of Europe. Writers such as Guy de Maupassant (1850–93), Stéphane Mallarmé (1842–98) and Arthur Rimbaud (1854–91) flourished in this centre of avant-garde culture. After the First World War, Paris attracted even more cultural figures from around the world including the exiled Russian composer Igor Stravinsky (1882–1971) and Spanish painters Pablo Picasso (1881–1973) and Salvador Dalí (1904–89).

Sensuality was condoned if not encouraged in Paris and among those drawn there, as much by the city's reputation for sexual freedom as for its cultural innovation was a group of wealthy American lesbians. This was nothing new for even before the moral tolerance brought by the French Revolution (1789–99) Paris had been a magnet for lesbians. All-female clubs, such as the Order of Anandryns, were known to have flourished in the 1780s; its members were rumoured to have included such aristocratic women as the Marquise Terracenes, wife of the Attorney General under Louis XVI, and the celebrated actresses Sophie Arnould (1744–1803) and Françoise Raucourt (1756–1815) of the *Comédie Française*, who often fought over their male and female lovers. Raucourt, in particular, was bold and unequivocal in her lesbianism.

This Sapphic environment grew throughout the 19th century and made Paris the unrivalled lesbian capital of Europe. Activity was particularly prevalent in the bohemian Montmartre district where cross-dressing was legally permitted as long as a woman had a special permit issued by the local police. The most spectacular and unambiguous display of lesbianism was the Mardi Gras Ball held annually in the Latin Quarter, when cross-dressing women mingled with young men costumed as pageboys.

By the end of the 19th century, lesbian life was an everyday scene on the streets of Montmartre with many cafes and restaurants having an almost exclusively female clientele. These venues also attracted male voyeurs, often wealthy tourists, keen to experience the titillation of seeing amorous women together. This relaxed and sensual feminine lifestyle featured in many of the paintings and drawings of the Parisian demi-monde by Henri de Toulouse-Lautrec (1864–1901). The city's reputation as a place where lesbian women could escape the censure of their own societies and openly express their sexuality proved particularly attractive in the first quarter of the 20th century to some American women who had the financial resources to maintain a prosperous lifestyle in exile.

One of the first American lesbians attracted to the city was the poet Natalie Clifford Barney (1876–1972), who established a literary salon at her home on the Left Bank. Born in 1876 in Dayton, Ohio, Barney was the daughter of a rich industrialist. At the age of six, she had met Oscar Wilde at New York's Long Beach Hotel when he was touring America. Both Barney and her mother were deeply impressed by the sophisticated representative of European culture.

Barney was to prove a rebellious and unconventional member of American society, often mounted astride her horse rather than riding side-saddle as propriety required at the time. At 16, she fell in love with a school friend, Eva Palmer, and they spent an idyllic summer together in Bar Harbor in Maine, running naked in the woods and playing at nymphs and shepherds. When their horrified families discovered these antics, both girls were sent off to separate boarding schools in disgrace. Barney later claimed that by the age of 12, she definitely knew that she was lesbian and was determined to escape the strictures of upper-class American society and 'live openly, without hiding anything'.

At the age of 24, she left America for near-permanent exile in Europe where, in 1899, she saw the famous courtesan Liane de Pougy (1869–1950) at a dance hall in Paris. Entranced by her beauty, Barney went to de Pougy's house the next day dressed in a theatrical costume and announced that she was de Pougy's page of love sent by Sappho to serve her. Charmed by her boldness, de Pougy embarked on a short affair with Barney and used it as the inspiration for *Sapphic Idyll*, a novel that scandalized Paris but was reprinted 69 times in its first year alone. However, Barney's determination to 'rescue' her mistress from her life as a courtesan was not appreciated by the bisexual de Pougy and the relationship soon floundered.

With characteristic drive and energy, Barney soon replaced her lost love with the poet Pauline Tarn (1877–1909), better known by her pen name Renée Vivien. This proved to be a far more productive relationship, inspiring both women to write of their emotions, using the conventions of courtly love. Together they studied classical Greek so that they could read Sappho's poems in the original and each wrote a play about the Greek poet. Having parted company, in 1904 Barney produced the poem 'I Remember' in a successful attempt to win Vivien back. Reconciled, they travelled to the island of Lesbos, where they considered starting a school of poetry for women, as Sappho herself had done 2,500 years earlier.

When the relationship finally ended Barney returned to her home at Neuilly near Paris to begin what was to be her life's work of establishing a modern literary salon in the grand 18th-century style. Literature was given pride of place on 'Fridays', when the salon convened and many of the leading writers of the age were invited to attend.

The playwright Joan Schenkar (b.1952) described Barney's salon as a place 'where lesbian assignations and appointments with academics could coexist in a kind of cheerful, cross-pollinating, cognitive dissonance'. The guests avoided any form of masculine attire in favour of flowing Greek robes. Many of the most prominent artistic figures of the age made their way to the salon at Neuilly, including the exotic dancer and spy Mata Hari (1876–1917), who rode into the garden mounted on a white horse and 'dressed' as Lady Godiva. This event, together with an outdoor performance of her play about Sappho which contained scenes of semi-nudity and females embracing each other, led to complaints from her landlord. Outraged by the man's lack of appreciation of the finer points of Sapphic aesthetics, Barney promptly gave up the house and moved closer into the city.

Her new home in the Rue Jacob was appropriately at the heart of the more tolerant and traditionally bohemian Latin Quarter of Paris. Until the early 1960s she held weekly sessions there welcoming many of the great literary figures of the age, including Ezra Pound (1885–1972), T. S. Eliot (1888–1965), Jean Cocteau (1889–1963), Ford Madox Ford (1873–1939), Somerset Maugham (1874–1965), F. Scott Fitzgerald (1896–1940), Sinclair Lewis (1885–1951), Sherwood Anderson (1876–1941), Thornton Wilder (1897–1975) and dozens more. Lesbian authors received a particularly warm welcome not least Marguerite Radclyffe Hall, author of the most famous lesbian novel ever written, *The Well of Loneliness*. Banned in Britain since its publication in 1928, Radclyffe Hall's book called for greater tolerance for what she described as 'sexual inverts'. However, for Barney there was no need for such condescension; she was proudly and confidently lesbian and saw no need to apologize either for her sexuality or her political opinions. Her proximity to the First World War had led her to believe that war was 'involuntary and collective suicide ordained by man' and that men 'father death as women mother life, with courage and without choice'.

Over the years Barney formed relationships with many women but none more poignantly than that with Dolly Wilde (1895–1941), the niece of Oscar who, like her unfortunate uncle, was doomed to a life of unfulfilled promise and ultimate self-destruction. Although famous for having inherited much of her uncle's wit,

Dolly was never able to emulate him in producing written work of any worth. Only her letters describing life in Paris at the time, reveal what she might have achieved as a writer if she had more self-control. Drifting from one crisis to another she was faithfully supported by Barney during her addiction to alcohol and heroin. Barney coped with her occasional attempts at suicide and financed the efforts at rehab, only to see her eventually become dependent on the sleeping drug paraldehyde. Suffering from cancer and separated from Barney, Dolly died of a drug overdose in 1941.

Barney's own source of support during the latter difficult years of dealing with Dolly Wilde was the American painter Romaine Brooks (1874–1970), who was to be her lover for 40 years. Brooks brought a terrible legacy to the relationship from the experience of her miserable childhood. Unloved and neglected by a wealthy, spoilt and unbalanced mother, Brooks was made the scapegoat for her mother's constant depression and inability to cope with life. Not surprisingly these experiences caused Brooks to develop a profound sense of loneliness. The damage was compounded by her mother dressing her in her elder brother's clothes and treating her as a second son. She concluded that she could no longer tolerate her six-year-old daughter at any price and left her to be looked after by a laundress in New York City. In spite of the dreadful treatment she had received and inheriting a vast fortune, when her mother died in 1902 she wrote, 'the deaths of my mother and brother [within the space of a year] had not liberated me mentally and I felt that some part of me still remained with them'.

However, the money did give her the freedom to divorce the man she had married, the homosexual pianist John Ellingham Brooks. Their marriage of convenience had lasted only a few months and served merely as a smokescreen for John Brooks after his affair with the 16-year-old Somerset Maugham. Free at last, Brooks went to London, where in 1904 she took a studio in London's Tate Street and began painting in earnest. The following year she moved to Paris and held a successful solo exhibition of the nudes and portraits that made clear her lesbian identity. Her love life became highly complicated when she became the lover of the

Italian fascist poet Gabriele d'Annunzio (1863–1938), at the same time as having a lesbian affair with the Russian ballet dancer Ida Rubenstein (1885–1960).

Perhaps as a consequence of her awful childhood in which she was a helpless victim, Romaine Brooks was attracted to the idea of herself as a woman of action and an apostle of such new and aggressive art movements as Italian Futurism. She was drawn to the Italian dictator Benito Mussolini (1883–1945) and his vision of a totalitarian state that embraced every activity including the arts. This vision of a fascist society could offer certainty to someone who was as insecure and chaotic as Brooks. To the illusory comfort of her belief in fascism, Brooks now added the stability of her long-term relationship with Natalie Barney. Although she came to dislike the artificiality of salon life and Barney was unfaithful, their love affair was a long and mutually beneficial one. Brooks also benefited from Barney's salons for they provided her with badly needed patrons. Her paintings of famous salon members gained her a reputation as a portraitist of considerable ability. In one picture she depicted Barney as an Amazon, whereas in another Una Troubridge, Marguerite Radclyffe Hall's lover, was shown as a male dandy with bobbed hair and a monocle. In 1967, towards the end of their lives in exile together, Barney revealed to Brooks that she had been having an affair with another woman for the past seven years. Devastated by the confession, Brooks ended the relationship and died alone three years later at the age of 96.

Yet the most famous of all the lesbian exiles was another American writer, Gertrude Stein, who without the benefit of the social graces of Natalie Barney's salons became one of the most important catalysts in the development of modern art and literature. The youngest child of German–Jewish immigrants Daniel and Amelia Stein, she was three years old when her family moved from Pennsylvania to Vienna and then on to Paris. These early years in Europe were to have a profound effect on her. Highly intelligent and an excellent philosophy student under Henry James's elder brother William, Stein decided to study medicine and enrolled at Johns Hopkins University in Baltimore. However, after the sophistication and historic heritage of Europe, American society proved too provincial for Stein and she swiftly abandoned her studies in favour of returning to Europe. Conveniently, in 1904 she was able to join her elder brother Leo in Paris at 27 Rue de Fleurus. Gertrude went to Paris not knowing that she would not set foot upon American soil again for the next 30 years.

Leo Stein was an avid follower of modern art and bought paintings that would form the basis of one of the most important private art collections of the 20th century. In partnership with Gertrude, he began filling the walls of every room in their apartment with pictures by Picasso (1881–1973), Renoir (1841–1919), Gauguin (1848–1903), Cezanne (1839–1906) and other contemporary artists. The Steins also became generous hosts to many of the leading artists and writers living in Paris. Pablo Picasso became a particularly close friend and he painted an iconic portrait of Gertrude in 1905. The Steins' growing collection was funded by the considerable wealth of their family in America. When, in 1904, they suddenly received an unexpected windfall of an extra 8,000 francs they used the money to purchase Gauguin's 'Sunflowers' and 'Three Tahitians', as well as acquiring Cézanne's 'Bathers' and two more Renoirs.

Before arriving in Paris, Gertrude Stein's experience of lesbianism had been a great disappointment. She had met her first lover, May Bookstaver, while studying at Johns Hopkins Medical School in the early 1890s. Unfortunately Bookstaver was also involved with another woman and the romantic triangle that ensued caused Stein great emotional pain. She managed to channel the traumatic experience into a novel *QED* that Stein kept secret and it was only published four years after her death. However, on 8 September 1907, Stein's life changed dramatically when she met a fellow American, Alice B. Toklas, who was touring Europe with her lesbian lover. There was an immediate rapport between the two women and Gertrude soon persuaded Toklas to move in with her. They would remain together until Gertrude's death in 1946. So began one of the most fascinating and productive female relationships since the Ladies of Llangollen, with Alice acting as Gertrude's companion and cultural factotum. When Leo returned to America, Alice took over his role in helping Gertrude manage the art collection and the most famous intellectual salon in Paris, the meeting place for avant-garde writers and artists. Stein made an enormous contribution to contemporary art for she not only collected but also helped launch the careers of both Henri Matisse (1869–1954) and Pablo Picasso.

The influence of the avant-garde can also be seen in her own experimental writing. Her first important book *Three Lives* was published two years before she met Alice. In it she began to develop the fractured style of prose that has been described as being as strange and as fresh to the reader's ear as cubist paintings were to the viewer's eye. Most readers, however, found her style far too dense and difficult to comprehend. It was only with the publication of her most famous work in 1933, *The Autobiography of Alice B Toklas*, that Stein was able to reach a wider audience and in the process transform Alice and herself into the best-known literary celebrities of the day.

When war came in 1914 they left Paris to escape the widely predicted bombing raids by Zeppelin airships that never materialized. After visiting the philosopher Alfred North Whitehead (1861–1947) in England, they decided that their flight had been unnecessary and quietly returned to Paris. Gertrude decided they must do something to help the war effort in their adopted country and she enlisted them both in the American Fund for French Wounded. At Stein's own expense, a large Ford automobile was shipped from America and fitted out like a truck from which they could deliver supplies to hospitals around Paris. This practical gesture of support earned them the gratitude of the French government and they were both decorated after the war.

Returning to their undamaged home in the Rue de Fleurus, they reopened their salon and Stein continued her writing. Her work began to take on the more openly lesbian stance that she had begun as early as 1900 when she published a series love poems to women under her own name. The new writing was much bolder and championed feminism, paganism and pacifism. Her 1922 story *Miss Furr and Miss Skeene* is one of the first 'coming out' works of lesbianism ever published. It uses the word 'gay' over 100 times and is perhaps the first printed use of the word in reference to same-sex relationships.

As their celebrity grew, the ladies travelled back to New York for the premiere of *Four Saints in Three Acts* with music by Virgil Thomson (1896–1989) and for which Stein had written the libretto. Again the work broke new ground as it featured an all-black cast of singers. Before returning to France, Stein gave several lectures at the University of Chicago. During one of these she made the famous statement always associated with her name 'a rose is a rose is a rose is a rose.' The unlikely celebrities toured the country, making more than 40 appearances and visiting old friends they had made in Paris including F. Scott Fitzgerald (1896–1940) and his wife Zelda (1900–48), Sherwood Anderson (1876–1941), Thornton Wilder (1897–1975), Charlie Chaplin (1889–1977), and many more.

As the Second World War (1939–45) approached, Toklas and Stein decided to remain in France and face the danger of being American Jews in a country occupied by the German Nazis. Living discreetly in various country houses around Belley in rural France under the nominal protection of Marshall Pétain (1856–1951) and his Vichy government, they remained undetected until the end of the war. To their great delight, when they returned in August 1944 to their house in Paris they found that the entire collection of the near priceless paintings had been left untouched by the Germans. Old friends soon drifted back to the city and the couple resumed their old life. However, a few months after the war ended Stein was on her way to give a lecture to American troops in Brussels when she collapsed with severe abdominal pains. She had advanced cancer of the colon but managed to survive another seven months before dying in a Paris hospital in July 1946. As she was about to be wheeled into emergency surgery just before her death, Stein asked the enigmatic question 'What is the answer?' Receiving no reply, she continued 'In that case ... what is the question?'

Stein's lesbian relationship with Toklas was undoubtedly important in bringing lesbianism into the open. Certainly Stein's book *The Autobiography of Alice B. Toklas* is the most famous documentation of early 20th-century lesbianism, as well as being a truly avant-garde work of literature. The innovative format of having her lover's voice tell her story allows Stein to experiment with the conventional boundaries between author, narrator, and subject. Often the reader has difficulty discovering where Stein ends and Toklas begins and vice versa.

No account of the extraordinary contribution that exiled American lesbians made to French and European culture would be complete without recording the achievements of the publisher Sylvia Beach (1887–1962). Escaping the strict Protestant morality of the family parsonage in Princeton, New Jersey, shortly before the First World War, Beach travelled throughout Italy and Spain before serving with the Red Cross in Serbia. When the war ended, she settled in Paris and fell in love with the literary scene, attending readings by such avant-garde authors as André Gide, Paul Valéry (1871–1945) and Jules Romains (1885–1972).

While researching at the Bibliothèque Nationale, Beach came across the name of Adrienne Monnier, who ran a bookshop in the rue de l'Odéon in the heart of the Latin Quarter. Intrigued by the idea of a woman running her own business, she visited the shop and found its owner to be a plump, fair-haired, young woman wearing a garment that resembled a cross between a peasant's dress and a nun's habit. There was an immediate attraction between the two women and a love affair began that lasted until Monnier's suicide in 1955. Beach was fascinated by Monnier's courage at being the first woman to sell books in Paris and for championing innovative modern writing. Admiration provoked a desire to emulate, and Beach decided to go back to New York and start a similar shop promoting French literature. This proved impossible for she had only US $3,000 of capital, but with Monnier's help she returned to Paris and opened her own English-language bookstore and lending library. The business, Shakespeare and Company, was first located in tiny premises in the Rue Dupuytren but quickly attracted many French and American readers.

As the shop flourished more space was needed and, in May 1921, Beach moved Shakespeare and Company to 12 rue de l'Odéon, directly opposite Adrienne Monnier's own bookshop, La Maison des Amis des Livres. In the interwar period, these shops became the most famous bookstores in Paris and the centre of French-Anglo-Irish-American literary life in Paris with Ernest Hemingway (1899-1961) and Ezra Pound (1885-1972) being regular customers. For aspiring authors both premises acted as clubhouse, library, post office, publishing house and even bank.

Beach's crowning achievement was to publish what is arguably the greatest novel of the 20th century – James Joyce's *Ulysses*. At the time no other publisher in the Western world was prepared to handle a work that was already infamous for its supposed obscenity. An indefatigable champion of all new writing, Beach found publishers and translators for other authors, too. She also provided her customers with readings by some of the most important literary figures of the day, such as T. S. Eliot (1888-1965), Paul Valery, André Gide and André Maurois (1885-1967). Monnier and Beach translated into French many important essays and poems, including Eliot's seminal 'The Love Song of J. Alfred Prufrock'.

Although Adrienne Monnier remained her principal lover, Beach had several affairs with other women over the years. However, when Monnier began a brief affair with another woman in 1936, Beach was devastated and ended their physical relationship. They remained friends and dined together every evening until Monnier's suicide. Neither woman ever discussed their relationship with outsiders but their professional achievement was outstanding and they made a unique contribution to the course of modern literature.

Among those encouraged by Beach's example and inspired by the brilliance of James Joyce's experimental writing was the poet Djuna Barnes (1892-1982), yet another wealthy American drawn to Paris by the culture and internationalism of the city. Barnes left

New York for Paris in 1920 and spent the next 20 years there in self-imposed exile from America. Culture was one attraction and the tolerant lesbian social life of the city another. Barnes immediately became part of the established Sapphic life of the city that was dominated by Natalie Barney, Gertrude Stein and Peggy Guggenheim (1898–1979).

Far more humorous in character than the established lesbian hostesses, she satirized their social and literary pretensions in her first major work, *Ladies Almanack* (1928). The book deals with the difficulties of being a lesbian in a sophisticated society as experienced by Dame Musset, – a character based on Barney – who combines a genuine desire to help other women with ludicrously aristocratic pretensions. The book was a critical success but Barnes was now drinking alcohol to excess. The problem was compounded when she met and fell in love with her fellow American expatriate Thelma Wood (1901–1970). Described by Barnes as 'a tall, handsome, hard-drinking woman', Wood was a sculptor and silverpoint artist. For eight years they had a passionate if volatile relationship, although monogamy did not come naturally to Wood who took to touring the Paris cafes looking for casual sex with either men or women. Wood eventually formed a relationship with Henriette Metcalf, a friend of the writer Colette and Barnes finally broke off the affair.

As miserable as she was, Barnes still managed to produce her second novel and acknowledged masterpiece *Nightwood*, the story of the doomed homosexual and heterosexual loves of five characters. The book was inspired by her traumatic relationship with Wood and was praised by such eminent critics as T. S. Eliot.

Paris had lost its attraction for Djuna Barnes, however, and soon after the affair with Wood she moved to England. At the outbreak of the Second World War in 1939, Barnes ended her exile and returned to New York where she lived a reclusive life of poverty in Greenwich Village. Her only financial support came from the wealthy Peggy Guggenheim, with whom she had an affair and who claimed that Barnes was drinking a bottle of whisky a day. During these years Barnes shunned interviews and even correspondence with her friends from the old days, although she did write one last letter to Natalie Barney when in her seventies saying 'Of course I think of the past and of Paris, what else is there to remember?' Janet Flanner, who reported for the *New Yorker* magazine on life in the city between the wars, wrote that Djuna Barnes was the most significant woman writer in Paris in the 1920s.

While most of the American lesbians in Paris were there primarily for the culture, they were unable to avoid the fast-changing political climate of the times. With Europe polarized between fascism and communism, the expatriates discovered that they could not avoid being drawn into the political turmoil. Some like Djuna Barnes, Sylvia Beach and poet Hilda Doolittle (1886–1961), a lover of Eleanor Roosevelt (1884–1962), remained faithful to their youthful idealism and left-wing sympathies. Others, such as Romaine Brooks, Gertrude Stein and Natalie Barney, found themselves increasingly sympathetic towards the new totalitarian systems that were emerging and especially Mussolini's regime in Italy. Among Il Duce's more vociferous supporters was Marguerite Radclyffe Hall, who even moved to Rome to be near him. She had as little sympathy with socialism as she had with feminism and the only radical aspect of her life was her lesbian sexuality. Her admiration for the Italian dictator was shared by Romaine Brooks, who also spent the war in Italy. A close friend of fascist poet Gabriele d'Annunzio, Brooks spent the war years in Italy and maintained an implicit belief in the virtues of Mussolini. When he was arrested in 1943 she lamented that with his imprisonment, 'the dream of a unified Europe collapses and the nightmare is reinforced by the steady advance of the Bolshevik army'.

Barney, too, shared this admiration of fascist Italy and moved her salon to Florence rather than risk the dangers of being in England during the Blitz. Whatever their commitment to culture, none of these women showed genuine concern for the injustices and brutalities of Italian Fascism or Nazi Germany.

Yet perhaps the most curious reaction of all was that of Gertrude Stein, who appears to have been that strangest of creatures, an anti-Semitic Jew. She even claimed to be scared of Jews declaring in words that could have been uttered by Hitler himself 'I believe they hate us and they want to cause a European war, then a revolution to destroy us completely.' Declaring such unambiguous support for the anti-Semites may explain why Stein managed to escape arrest and deportation as a Jew under first the Vichy regime, then under German-controlled France. Perhaps choosing to reject her own Jewishness was not merely an act of self-preservation but also a gesture of modernism that saw an accident of birth as having no relevance to her career as a writer.

GAY LIFE IN THE PRE-1945 WORLD

While Paris and Italy remained the historic centres of homosexual enlightenment, by 1900 other European countries had begun relaxing the worst of their anti-sodomy laws. In Britain, however, the *Labouchere Amendment* of 1885, which prohibited gross indecency between males, remained in force, and in America the anti-sodomy laws were largely a matter of state rather than federal jurisdiction.

A new era of tolerance appeared in Russia following the revolution of 1917. Under the Tsarist monarchy, sodomy had been treated as a serious crime governed by the Russian *Criminal Code* of 1832. Those convicted could, in theory, be exiled to Siberia for at least four years. Yet pursuing homosexuals was never a priority for the Tsarist police, who were more concerned with suppressing revolutionary activity and maintaining the monarchy. The tactics of surveillance and entrapment that had been used in other European countries to catch sodomites were largely ignored in Russia. Occasionally in some isolated areas, old sexual customs bearing a strange resemblance to the Greek Love of the ancient world could be found. One example was the secret Skoptsy sect, which was based as much on commercial interest as sexual pleasure. An older merchant would adopt a younger assistant as his lover and heir. He would then tutor him in business skills and pass on the benefits of his own experience, much as the Greek warriors had passed on military skills to their younger lovers. When the older man died, his lover would inherit the business and then repeat the process with a younger lover of his own. Organizations such as the Skoptsy had been common in Russia since the 14th century and reveal a society more concerned with economic survival than artificial morality. In wider Russian society, there was generally a tolerance of homosexuality, particularly among members of the aristocracy, whose power under the Tsar was not subject to any great moral pressure from the Orthodox Church. In 1903 politician Vladimir Nabokov, father of the writer of the same name and a founder of the Constitutional Democratic party, published an article on the legal status of gays in Russia in which he argued that the state should not interfere in private sexual relationships. The period between the revolutions of 1905 and 1917 may have been the Silver Age in Russian literature, but it was also a golden age for Russian homosexuals. Many important figures led openly gay lives, including several members of the Imperial Court and a large community of artists and musicians, among them the greatest figure in Russian ballet, the impresario Sergei Diaghilev (1872–1929).

However, exiled revolutionaries Karl Marx (1818–83) and Friedrich Engels (1820–95) were among the homophobes, constantly condemning same-sex relationships in spite of their commitment to 'socialist brotherly love'. Engels was known to have detested 'the abominable practice of sodomy' and thought that his cherished working class must be kept free of such contamination. In Engels's opinion, if a working man was discovered to be a homosexual it was not his own fault. He was certain to have been recruited and corrupted by a member of the despised bourgeoisie. Nor, according to the revolutionaries, was lesbianism compatible with the true revolutionary spirit. Most importantly, sexuality, in general, was an annoying distraction from the real task in hand, that of overthrowing governments and bringing about a socialist paradise. It is perhaps surprising, therefore, that when revolution did finally come to Russia in 1917 the sexual warnings of Marx and Engels had been completely forgotten. Their Marxist puritanism had been replaced by the principles of universal moral freedom that had begun with the Enlightenment and the French Revolution of more than a century earlier.

When the first *Bolshevik Criminal Code* of 1922 was published, it contained no mention of sodomy as a crime and even the words 'sodomy', along with 'fornication', were absent from the law books.

From now on, it seemed that sex that did not involve violence, social disruption or the corruption of the young would be considered a private matter.

Although homosexuality was openly tolerated through greater Russia, it was not given the same status as heterosexual marriage. Most Bolshevik leaders returning from exile in Germany and other European countries agreed with scientists of the day that homosexuality was a medical condition, a hormonal anomaly that would one day be controlled and quite possibly even eradicated. To support this argument, experiments, which were the predecessors of the horrific ones later carried out by Nazi prison camp doctors, were undertaken by Russian scientists. One involved the implantation of sheep and pig ovary sections into the breast of a 28-year-old lesbian 'patient'. On a more positive note, the traditional persecution of homosexuals that was being pursued in Britain at the time was to the Soviet Bolsheviks irrational, reactionary and, worst of all, irredeemably bourgeois.

As the idealism of the revolution faded, it was replaced with the inevitable cynicism of everyday government. The suspicion of gay men in public life returned and was repoliticized in a way that suited the Soviet State. Homosexuality was associated with what was perceived as the most dangerous threat to the state – the rise of Fascism. This idea was eagerly taken up by Josef Stalin (1879–1953) when he replaced Lenin (1870–1924) as supreme ruler. With Stalin's full approval, in 1934, Maxim Gorky (1868–1936) famously stated in Pravda: 'destroy the homosexuals and Fascism will disappear'. That became the credo of the Soviet State and his words were immediately, and ominously, endorsed by the head of the NKVD secret police, G. Iagoda, who specifically linked homosexuality to espionage and counter-revolutionary activities.

The persecution of potentially traitorous homosexuals now became part of the campaign against anti-Soviet elements in general. Such condemnation may also have been intended to remind the world of the 'moral purity' of Soviet life and its priority to defend heterosexual marriage, although it astonished such Western liberals as the English writer Christopher Isherwood, who thought Stalin's action a betrayal of the basic principles of Communist freedom. To this end, abortion would also soon be banned and divorce made more difficult and expensive to obtain. The result was that female freedom was curtailed in the same way as male homosexuality. This was seen as a vital part of the state initiative to increase the declining birth rate as the Soviet Union prepared to face its political enemies, particularly Fascist Italy and Nazi Germany, on the battlefield. Revolutionary policy was abandoned and female prostitutes were arrested and deported to rural work camps. Sodomy was made a crime for the first time since 1917 and male prostitutes were made particular targets for persecution.

Mass round-ups of known or suspected gays began in 1933 in Moscow, Leningrad, Kharkov, Odessa and other Soviet cities. Many of those arrested were the leading creative artists of Soviet society – men such as the film director Sergei Paradjanov (1924–90) and the poet Gennady Trifonov – and all those convicted were exiled to the Gulags of Siberia. Many gay artists swiftly married to present a respectable public face, much as the closet homosexuals had done in Victorian England.

One of the most high-profile victims was Sergei Eisenstein (1898–1948), one of the greatest film-makers in the history of world cinema. Always careful to support the party line and to obtain the personal approval of Stalin before filming any controversial scenes, Eisenstein presented the external image of a loyal party member. Privately, he constantly struggled to repress his homosexual feelings and once claimed to friends that 'if it wasn't for Marx, Lenin and Freud, I would have been a new Oscar Wilde'. Yet, even those beacons of moral rectitude could not save Eisenstein from a risky sexual encounter with a young man while on location filming *Qué Viva Mexico*. When news of this misdemeanour reached Moscow, Stalin was furious and ordered Eisenstein to marry as soon as he returned home. This harrying of Russian intellectuals makes the sympathy for the Soviet Union that many English homosexuals had, including the Cambridge spies Guy Burgess and Kim Philby, all the more inexplicable. While embracing the ideals of Communism, they ignored the brutal homophobia of a system that suppressed personal freedom and intellectual liberty.

The actual numbers of homosexuals tried and sent into Siberian exile during Stalin's regime is still not known but the practice continued after his death and by the 1980s about 1,000 men were still being arrested every year. Throughout the years of Stalin's regime, the Soviet Union had the largest population of incarcerated men in the world and among them was a despised class of individuals known as *opushchennye*, or the 'degraded ones'. Their fate was to serve the sexual needs of the rest. The degraded ones included not just men convicted of sodomy but offenders who had lost at cards or offended a more powerful prisoner.

The few surviving Moscow court records from the 1930s to the 1950s show that, despite more stringent laws, the police were unsuccessful in eliminating the homosexual subculture from Russia's capital. Even at the height of the Great Terror at the end of the 1930s, men were still congregating to meet each other in well-established cruising spots, such as the streets and public toilets at Nikitskie Gate in the centre of Moscow. Given the ferocity of state terror, the fact that these men took such risks suggests a remarkable form of quiet social disobedience.

In Germany, gay people fared better after the First World War, in the years when the Weimar Republic existed (1919–33). Born of the bitterness of Germany's defeat in the First World War, the Weimar Republic, the predecessor of Hitler's Nazi regime (1933–45), was a fragile attempt at democracy. Surviving just 14 years from its creation in 1919 in the provincial city of Weimar, the democratic republic was based on a system of universal suffrage under which the people directly elected a president for a seven-year term. The president then appointed a chancellor, who had to be approved by the Reichstag, to administer the country.

The war had polarized people into supporting parties of the extreme left and extreme right who were dedicated to overthrowing the government and establishing their own totalitarian regimes. As well as serious political instability the new government also had to cope with a society destabilized by war and economic crisis. Yet none of these problems prevented the city of Berlin from becoming the gay capital of Europe in the years between the two world wars. In spite of the constant political friction, social life in Berlin was remarkably relaxed and attractive, a place where gay men and lesbians could live relatively open lives and take advantage of a currency exchange rate that made the cost of living in Berlin the lowest in Western Europe. The greatest attraction of all, however, was the vibrant cultural life of the city that had, albeit temporarily, replaced that of Paris, making it a magnet for artists, writers and musicians from all over Europe and the United States.

For many gay people in the 1930s the liberal climate of the Weimar Republic appeared to offer the best prospect of life in a society free from the homophobic prejudice that still pervaded the United States and other North European countries. One lesbian drawn to the city was the Anglo-German psychiatrist Charlotte Wolff (1897-1986), who was later imprisoned by the Nazis for cross-dressing. She wrote that 1930s Berlin:

> ... had become a paradise for homosexuals. The city drew people from all over the world who wanted to enjoy the freedom of sexual expression which their own country continued to deny them.

There were so many gays exiled in the city that a whole community had become established. There were dozens, if not hundreds, of places of assignation where gays of either sex could meet. These ranged from clubs, restaurants and hotel lobbies to the premises of the Young Men's Christian Association. There were also bars where ex-soldiers gathered and many of these, who were either bisexual or homosexual, were prepared to provide sex in return for money or even a good meal. Healthy outdoor living was the fashion of the day and walking and cycling in city parks or leaving the city for the summer to visit country inns or gardens became the common pursuit.

The most important observer of this gay activity was the social scientist Magnus Hirschfeld (1868–1935), who was known as 'The Einstein of Sex'. A follower of early homosexual theorist Karl Heinrich Ulrichs, who believed that homosexuals had female souls trapped within male bodies, and vice versa for lesbians, Hirschfeld was an important theorist of sexuality and the most prominent advocate of homosexual emancipation at the time. Hirschfeld remains one of the most impressive figures of the period – a man dedicated to the Enlightenment principles of rationality and the scientific investigation of human sexuality.

As a Jew living in a historically anti-Semitic country, Hirschfeld urged gays to accept their sexuality and to become involved in a universal campaign for emancipation. He was convinced that only a scientific understanding of sexuality would lead to a society tolerant of sexual minorities. Hirschfeld contended that human beings are unique composites made up of different proportions of masculinity and femininity that can alter, which makes it impossible to rigidly categorize human sexuality.

During the course of his investigation, he estimated that he had spoken to more than 30,000 men and women and he had come to the conclusion that complete sexual honesty was the only way to achieve freedom. As if in support of his own theories, he maintained a bisexual private life. In 1899 Hirschfeld began publishing *The Yearbook of Intermediate Sexual Types*, the world's first scientific journal of sex that contained articles on homosexuality in primitive societies. In July 1919 he opened the Institute for Sexual Science, the forerunner of such organizations as the Kinsey Institute in the United States.

As far as right-wing nationalists were concerned, Hirschfeld was not only an advocate of sodomy but also a Jew and he became an obvious target for their violence. He was first assaulted in the street in Munich in 1920; he suffered a fractured skull the following year and was still being beaten up a decade later. From 1929 onwards the Nazis, who were growing in power, began disrupting his lectures at the institute. He continued his research into the homosexual world of Berlin and estimated that there were more than 20 homosexual bars in the city centre alone. A moralist in many ways, Hirschfeld had little time for such establishments. He blamed them for the serious outbreaks of venereal disease in the city and believed they encouraged crime, particularly blackmail. The Berlin police came to a similar conclusion and kept these venues under careful observation while taking little action against the clientele.

At the same time, Adolf Brand, publisher of the first-ever gay magazine, *Der Eigene* (*The Special*), took an entirely different and more aggressive stance. These so-called 'Brandites', who preferred to see themselves as a breed of man superior even to heterosexuals, were the first modern believers in a form of aggressive gay pride. Their Community of the Special or 'CS' claimed that male homosexuality had been the foundation of every successful state in history and that gays were the elite force in any society. Their role models were the homosexual warriors of ancient Greece and in this they shared a curious similarity of belief to Lord Byron and A. J. Symonds. Modelling themselves on the military bands of Sparta, Thebes and Crete, they committed themselves to male-only sex and were driven by a 'thirst for a revival of Greek times and Hellenic standards of beauty after centuries of Christian barbarism'. However, there was a fundamental difference between the CS and the ancient Greeks, for rather than defending democracy they were attracted to the idea of a totalitarian state that would find its model in the Nazi regime of Adolf Hitler. It could even be argued that without the CS the Nazis would never have found so many willing recruits for their movement.

The German youth movement known as the *Wandervogel*, or Wandering Youth, had spontaneously arisen in the 1890s as a popular hiking and camping movement similar to the English and American Boy Scouts. From its early days, the *Wandervogel* was dominated and controlled by homosexuals of the CS. Its young members were indoctrinated with ideas of Greek paganism and taught to reject the Christian values of their Catholic and Lutheran parents. Their paramount belief was in the creation of a gay elite under a Führer or supreme leader.

The natural progression for many CS members in the late 1920s was to the *Sturm Abteilung* (SA), or 'brownshirts', whose leader was Ernst Röhm (1887–1934). Röhm was one of the few prosecuted for sodomy in 1930 under the laws of the Weimar Republic. Röhm envisaged a new social order in which gay people would be given the highest respect in a new totalitarian state and he flaunted his homosexuality in public and encouraged his followers do the same. By 1933 the SA outnumbered the regular German army and nearly all of its leaders were gay. As the historian H. R. Knickerbocker has pointed out, Röhm was the most powerful man in Germany and personally commanded a private army of 2,500,000 storm troopers. Without exception each of its units was commanded by a gay officer. In the SA, the ideal of masculine gay supremacy and a military state were fully realized. The organization was the very personification of masculinity with its camps, marches, rallies and focus on sport. To the socialist press, the fact that the SA was dominated by gays provided invaluable ammunition with which to attack the hypocrisy of the ascendant Nazis and their alleged emphasis on traditional family values. The *Munich Post* accused Röhm of participating in 'fornication that would make your hair stand on end' and of abusing unemployed young workers thus neatly linking two social issues of current concern in Germany. Parents, it argued, should dissuade their children from joining the SA as it was becoming a cesspit of moral depravity.

Hitler himself maintained a pragmatic view of the SA and its notorious homosexuality, choosing to see its ideal of perfectly bodied and athletic young storm troopers as the Siegfrieds of National Socialism, as portrayed by the director Leni Reifenstahl (1902–2003) in her stunning but frightening depiction of the 1934 Nuremberg Rally in the film *The Triumph of the Will*.

Meanwhile, many wealthy English homosexuals had exiled themselves in Berlin, including the poet W. H. Auden and his friend and lover, the novelist Christopher Isherwood. Auden, one of the most influential poets of the 20th century, was 20 when he first went to live in the city. He had recently graduated from Oxford and in spite of his homosexuality had decided to conform to social convention by becoming engaged. Troubled by a similar sexual conflict to the one that had affected A. J. Symonds about half a century earlier, Auden had undertaken a modern approach by deciding to embark on a course of psychoanalysis. Unfortunately, neither this nor a year of self-imposed celibacy brought any resolution to the problem. Had he remained in England, Auden might well have adopted the same heterosexual façade as Symonds and gone ahead with his plans to marry. However, lack of academic success and an early setback to his literary career prompted him to look further afield.

In spite of his promise as a poet, Auden had received a disappointing third-class degree in English at Oxford and his first collection of poems had been rejected. He had been attracted to several of his fellow undergraduates at Oxford but his lack of confidence in his own sexuality led to botched approaches and disappointment. Overwhelmed by this sense of failure, Auden was particularly receptive when his friend, Isherwood, wrote from Germany urging him to 'Come to Berlin, Berlin means boys'. This was the opportunity for Auden to explore his homosexuality without compromising his social or academic position. Within weeks of his arrival, Auden was writing to friends enthusing about Berlin's gay life, with its police-controlled male brothels and boys available for money in the bars and streets.

While Auden was still testing the gay waters of Berlin, Christopher Isherwood was already fully immersed in the pleasures of Berlin life. The newfound freedom in the new German republic had led to a mushrooming of bars, clubs, theatres and cabarets catering for gay men and women from all over Europe. In Isherwood's novel *The World in the Evening*, he describes how Berlin during the Weimar Republic far exceeded Paris in sexual freedom:

> *In Berlin, it wasn't enough merely to want sex; you were expected to specialize, to ask for a teen-age virgin, a 70-year-old woman, a girl with a whip and high boots, a transvestite, a policeman, a pageboy or a dog.*

Utterly captivated by the louche atmosphere, Isherwood realized that for the first time in his life he could live openly as a gay person and no longer be excluded from society. A visit to Magnus Hirschfeld's institute further encouraged his growing belief that he was part of a worldwide homosexual brotherhood that was seeking recognition and equality with mainstream heterosexual society. His English reserve, however, made him vulnerable to fits of giggling from embarrassment when at the Institute. He later acknowledged that his attitude towards Hirschfeld and his associates had been childish and inappropriate saying 'I laughed at them often, then. Now I see them as heroic and noble.'

Soon Auden and Isherwood were sharing their exile together as part of Berlin's rapidly growing expatriate and transient gay community, although their personal relationship was often acrimonious. Isherwood later claimed that Auden was both fascinated and repelled by his character, 'Wystan once told me almost admiringly that I was the cruellest and most unscrupulous person he had ever met.' Life in the city was to inspire Isherwood's second book, *The Memorial*, whose plot was described by the author as: 'in the deliciously prohibited world of Berlin in 1928 a World War aviator finds love in the arms of his muscular lover'.

The writers' immersion in the poverty-stricken world of working-class Berliners has often been seen as a gesture of left-wing solidarity by the two exiles. However, Peter Parker, Isherwood's biographer, thinks that they were motivated entirely by sexual pleasure and took full advantage of the impoverished young men they met. He caustically observes of Auden and Isherwood that 'the nearest either of them got to solidarity with the workers was sleeping with them'. Isherwood, in particular, was eagerly looking for 'rough trade', sexual partners without social pretensions who were often in it only for the money. Later, Isherwood told the American journalist Studs Terkel (1912–2008) that he found the lower class to be 'forthright and less tricky' and that his 'sexual colonialism' gave him a preference for lovers of 'not only another class, but another race.' In this he showed a great similarity with E. M. Forster and his preference for both the working-class and Indians.

When Auden and Isherwood were joined in Berlin by their friend, the bisexual poet Stephen Spender (1909–95), he, too, was enthralled by the homoerotic sight of the young male bodies on display in the parks, not realizing that many of these bronzed men would soon become ruthless and homophobic Nazi thugs. Spender's presence in Berlin, however, caused some annoyance to the cautious Isherwood who jealously resented him constantly taking photographs of himself and his boyfriend Heinz. Soon this sybaritic lifestyle would end and the Nazi newspaper – *Volkische Beobachter* – would condemn Weimar Berlin as 'a melting pot of everything that is evil – prostitution, drinking dens, cinemas, Marxism, Jews, strippers, negroes and all the vile offshoots of modern art'.

In the meantime Berlin remained the cultural magnet of Europe attracting writers, painters, musicians and film-makers from all over the Continent. All were entranced but sometimes repelled by the rootless modernity they discovered there. Such a seductive and louche atmosphere could not be found anywhere else at the time and was captured in the paintings of George Grosz (1893–1959), who documented Berlin low life as surely as Toulouse-Lautrec had done that of Paris 40 years earlier. These iconic images of Berlin decadence perfectly complemented Christopher Isherwood's prose in his novels *Goodbye to Berlin* and *Mr Norris Changes Trains*. Grosz generously acknowledged Isherwood's achievement as a foreigner in describing in words the transient spirit of Weimar Berlin, 'You are the first to really capture Berlin's atmosphere', Grosz wrote to him admiringly.

The cultural excitement of the city and the ready availability of casual sex captivated the young Englishmen whose allowances from England made them financially far better off than their working-class German boyfriends. As Isherwood wrote, perhaps cynically, 'Kisses and embraces, as always, had price tags attached to them but here the prices were drastically reduced to the cut throat competition of an overcrowded market.'

Having experienced such personal freedom neither Auden nor Isherwood would be inclined to consider ending their exile and returning to live full time in the confines of English society. Yet the dangers of sudden political change were obvious to everyone in Berlin as the social unrest increased and the Nazis became an ominous presence on the streets. Some of the exiled homosexuals appeared unaware of the imminent dangers they faced, one acquaintance of Isherwood's remarking how sexy the storm troopers looked in their tight-fitting uniforms. At first Isherwood, too, seemed unconcerned with the growing threat of the Nazis believing that even if it came to the worst he 'would not fall into the hands of the storm trooper: foreigners were dealt with by the police, who treated you with respect for your civil rights.' The worst that would happen, he supposed, would be a quiet expulsion from Germany. But when reminded that he had posed to his English friends as a dedicated opponent of Hitler and the Nazis, Isherwood's courage began to fail 'and he fancied he heard heavy wagons drawing up before the house in the middle of the night.'

When Adolf Hitler was elected German Chancellor in January 1933, a whole series of new laws reflecting Nazi beliefs and controlling moral behaviour were rapidly introduced.

Within days of Hitler being sworn in as Chancellor on 30 January 1933, every club or bar frequented by gays was closed down by the police and all their magazines banned. The police then began collecting the names and addresses of known gays as they had done with the Jews. These lists would later be collated and used to hunt down individuals who had contravened the new laws extending the definition of 'criminally indecent activities between men' to include any act that could be construed as homosexual. The onslaught against gays continued on 6 May 1933, when a mob of students and storm troopers invaded the Institute for Sexual Science in Berlin and removed its valuable collection of more than 12,000 books and 35,000 pictures. Four days later, the entire collection together with thousands of other so-called 'degenerate' works of literature were burned in the city centre. The attack was not motivated solely by the Nazi's new enmity against the gays of the SA, however. It was also an attempt to destroy evidence of Hitler's own murky sexual past. Hitler knew that Magnus Hirschfeld's Institute contained detailed records that could be damaging to himself and his inner circle. When he heard that the facility had been vandalized, Hirschfeld, who was lecturing in France at the time, decided not to return to Germany and went into exile.

Hitler now turned to the problem of dealing with Ernst Röhm and the SA because by June 1934 the SA was seen as a growing threat to the regular army's authority. Not only did the SA outnumber the army but Röhm had also alarmed army leaders by threatening to absorb it into the SA. The German high command appealed to Hitler to take action, convincing him that Röhm was a threat that had to be removed. Hitler, ever the opportunist, used the situation to strengthen his own position. He told army leaders that he would deal with Röhm and the other SA leaders, bringing the rank and file SA members under the control of the army. In return, the army would have to swear an oath of loyalty to Hitler. The deal was agreed and the 'Night of the Long Knives' commenced. On the night of 29 June 1934, units of Himmler's SS arrested the leaders of the SA and other political opponents such as Gregor Strasser (1892–1934), von Schleicher (1882–1934) and von Bredow (1884–1934). As a result at least 77 men were executed on charges of treason. Röhm was shot and many of the others bludgeoned to death.

As tolerance of homosexuality ended and repressive laws came into force, Isherwood gained an early experience of just how dangerous life under the Nazis would be. His current boyfriend, Heinz Neddermayer, was risking arrest for avoiding the military draft. Desperately Isherwood tried to get Heinz out of the country by paying a fellow gay exile, Gerald Hamilton, the large sum of £1,000 to arrange Mexican citizenship for him. Hamilton appears to have done little other than pocket the money himself and Heinz was arrested. Isherwood took his revenge by using Hamilton, a man once described as a rogue laced with poison, as the basis for the character of Arthur Norris in his satirical novel of Berlin life, *Mr Norris Changes Trains*. It was only later that Isherwood discovered Hamilton's appalling track record of deceit and swindling. He had even been imprisoned in England during the First World War for his 'openly expressed pro-German and anti-British sentiments' that provoked the British politician Horatio Bottomley (1860–1933) to demand that they 'Hang Hamilton'.

Under Hitler's regime the German courts could decide that simply having homosexual thoughts or intentions was sufficient for conviction. In 1936 Himmler established the Reich Central Office for Combating Abortion and Homosexuality, staffed by members of his own SS. At its head was Josef Meisinger, a typically brutal Nazi who was executed after the war for the atrocities that he committed in occupied Poland. Under Meisinger's orders the police could hold without trial anyone suspected of damaging the moral fibre of Germany by engaging in homosexual acts. Lesbians, however, were not considered a threat to Nazi racial policies and were generally left alone. Sometimes the Nazi authorities used the charge to discredit and undermine their political opponents. In 1935 a propaganda campaign against 'perverted priests' saw two show trials alleging rampant homosexuality in the priesthood, which were used to get rid of opponents in the Roman Catholic Church.

Meanwhile, in 1935, W. H. Auden made his own small contribution to thwarting the Nazis when he agreed to a marriage of convenience with Erika Mann (1905–69), the lesbian daughter of Thomas Mann (1875–1956), Germany's greatest living writer. She had asked Isherwood first but he had declined on the grounds that such an arranged marriage would deeply upset his elderly mother. So the job was left to Auden, for as the wife of a British citizen, Erika Mann would be entitled to a British passport that allowed her to leave Germany at any time. The following year she left with her father and homosexual brother, Klaus, for the United States, continuing her friendship with Auden while going her own sexual way. Neither of them ever bothered to apply for a divorce.

Both Auden and Isherwood had gained immeasurably as writers from their time in Berlin. Auden had seen his poetic career take off and he was clearly a rising star in the international literary world. Much of his work reflected his left-wing sympathies and warned of the growing dangers of totalitarianism. Some of the plays he wrote at the time, such as *The Dog Beneath the Skin*, *The Ascent of F6* and *On the Frontier*, were written in collaboration with Isherwood and won great critical acclaim. Gradually disillusionment with the ineffectiveness of socialism in the face of violent fascism set in, particularly after Auden reported as a journalist on the Spanish Civil War (1936–39) and he and Isherwood witnessed Japan's aggression in Manchuria. Europe seemed about to descend into chaos and war, and neither writer was committed enough to either their native country or international socialism to become involved in the forthcoming struggle. In 1939 they opted out by leaving Europe behind and sailing into exile in the United States. Their flight on the eve of the Second World War was seen by many as an act of cynical self-preservation that made a mockery of their political posturing. By choosing the safety of America they particularly shocked their many left-wing friends who had been their keenest supporters, although Isherwood at least was quite open about his own motives for leaving Europe when he wrote in his diary for 11 January 1940:

> *Am I afraid of being bombed? Of course, everybody is. But within reason I know I certainly wouldn't leave Los Angeles if the Japanese were to attack it tomorrow. No, it isn't that.... If I fear anything, I fear the atmosphere of the war, the power that it gives to all the things I hate – the newspapers, the politicians, the puritans, the scoutmasters, the middle-aged merciless spinsters. I fear the way I might behave, if I were exposed to this atmosphere. I shrink from the duty of opposition. I am afraid I should be reduced to a chattering enraged monkey, screaming back hate at their hate.*

But most gay people in Nazi Germany were not as lucky as Isherwood and Auden. On 4 April 1938, a dictate ordered that homosexuals be incarcerated in concentration camps and over the next seven years more than 100,000 men suspected of homosexuality were arrested, of whom half were convicted and sentenced to internal exile within the prison and concentration camp system. Most were thoroughly respectable citizens – their only crime was that they were attracted to other men, yet regardless of age or background each was forced to wear a pink triangle denoting sexual deviancy, while political prisoners wore red, habitual criminals green, gypsies black and so on. The pink triangle was seen as a badge of dishonour that earned the wearer particularly harsh treatment in camps, where an estimated 60 percent of homosexuals perished – far more than in any other Nazi-deemed 'anti-social' group. The worst and most degrading work was reserved for gays, such as slaving in the stone quarries at Flossenbürg or enduring the dangers of the Dora-Mittelbau underground rocket factory.

For some, their very homosexuality proved the means of survival because they could barter sexual favours with the Kapos who policed the camps in return for extra food or lighter work duties. Young, attractive men could take this route but for the rest the only alternative to an early death was to be castrated. This was generally offered at the time of conviction in return for a more lenient sentence. Another horror awaited anyone unlucky enough to come to the attention of the Nazi camp doctors who carried out 'scientific' experiments. At Buchenwald, SS physician Dr Carl Vaernet performed operations designed to convert men to heterosexuals by surgically inserting a capsule that released the male hormone testosterone.

There are no known statistics for the exact number of gays who died in the camps and after the war homosexual prisoners were not acknowledged as victims of Nazi persecution in the same way that the Jews, Gypsies and Slavs were. No memorial was ever built for them and no detailed evidence of their fate catalogued. When the war ended, the stigma continued under the Allied Military Government of Germany. All reparations were refused and some were even forced to complete their sentences regardless of the time they had spent in the camps. The justification for this was that these men were 'legally' convicted criminals although the judiciary that had punished them was part of the most tyrannical dictatorship in history. Even more inexplicably Paragraph 175 of the Nazi penal code that prohibited homosexual acts remained in force in the Federal Republic of West Germany and those convicted faced up to 5 years imprisonment. As late as 1957 the Federal Constitutional Court of West Germany, without a trace of remorse, not merely upheld the Nazi laws but even suggested that the penalty be doubled – to 10 years imprisonment. Only in 1969, more than two decades after the liberation, was it finally removed thus lifting the threat of arrest and imprisonment for Germany's gay population. It is only in recent years that these forgotten victims have come forward to testify to their suffering.

FROM EUROPE TO
THE UNITED STATES

The United States was a place of refuge for many exiled artists and writers, whether gay or heterosexual, escaping war-torn Europe. On arriving in New York in January 1939, W. H. Auden found other English gay friends already there, such as the pacifist composer Benjamin Britten (1913–76) and tenor Peter Pears (1910–86).

In California the few English writers present were already far outnumbered by the many exiled artists, writers and academics from Europe, among them Hans Hofmann (1880–1966), who was the nucleus of the Abstract Expressionist movement, and the Surrealist painters Pavel Tchelitchew (1898–1957) and Alfred Salmony (1890–1958). Homosexual academics from Europe also revitalized American higher education making Princeton University the centre of excellence for both arts and sciences and the medievalist, Ernst Kantorowicz (1895–1963), an openly gay member of the Stefan George circle, established an equally celebrated faculty at Berkeley.

For Auden the move to the United States was to have a profound significance in determining the future of his emotional life. After years of uncertainty about his homosexuality, followed by the excesses of Berlin, he found his first real soul mate in New York – a precocious 18-year-old poet from Brooklyn named Chester Kallman (1921–75). Although their sexual partnership ended after just two years, they were to spend the rest of Auden's life together.

Unlike his old lover Isherwood, Auden was unimpressed by the prospect of the bright sunshine and the brash lifestyle of Californian society and decided to remain in the East. Isherwood, with the West Coast still in mind, began his American career in New York before travelling on to Haverford, Pennsylvania, where he taught English to German refugees. Unlike Auden, he soon became disillusioned with

East Coast society and found the atmosphere of New York, in particular, almost as oppressive as Henry James had done a century earlier. Once again he moved on, this time to California and settled in the Santa Monica Canyon near Los Angeles, where he supported himself by working as a Hollywood screenwriter, mainly writing the dialogue for a series of undistinguished movies, few of which made it into production. Unlike his more committed fellow émigrés, such as Bertolt Brecht (1898–1956), who equated screenwriting with prostitution, Isherwood was quite happy working as a studio hack, any professional disappointment being compensated for by the vitality of Californian social life. Many other creative exiles were also in California, among them the Irish writer Gerald Heard (1889–1971) and the English actor Charles Laughton (1899–1962), both of whom were gay.

Heard was an old Californian hand, having arrived in 1937 with his friend, the novelist Aldous Huxley (1894–1963), and both became fascinated by the teachings of the Hindu monk Swami Prabhavananda, founder of the Vedanta Society of Southern California. Convinced that a new form of spiritual consciousness was the way ahead for mankind, Heard introduced Isherwood to the Vedanta Circle. This had been established in 1934 as a non-profit organization to promote harmony between Eastern and Western thought and 'to recognise the truth in all the great religions of the world'. Heard was a complex character; he had been a BBC announcer before turning to writing and philosophy. His most influential work, *Pain, Sex and Time*, is a distillation of many of the ideas associated with Vedanta, which argues that physical evolution in human beings has ceased and psychological evolution needs to take over. All those connected with the Vedanta Society believed that they could expand their consciousness by meditation and other intellectual techniques. Heard also helped lay the philosophical foundations for the emergent gay movement in California and, together with Isherwood and Huxley, became known as one of the 'British Mystical Expatriates of Southern California.'

California had long been the most sexually tolerant of American states – even though a law against sodomy had been part of its original criminal code in 1850, it was rarely enforced. During the Californian Gold Rush that coincided with the foundation of the State, men were thrown together by circumstance and often paired up sexually together with one or other taking on the female role for cooking, dancing or sex. San Francisco, in particular, retained the atmosphere of a boom town 'where anything goes' long after the Gold Rush ended. The city's Barbary Coast and Tenderloin districts earned a reputation for catering to sexual tourists. A report published on the Dash saloon in 1908 stated that female impersonators entertained customers and that 'homosexual sex could be purchased in booths for a dollar.' During the 1930s, just before Isherwood arrived, the association of homosexuality with effeminacy in the clubs had so increased that the mainstream show business magazine *Variety* was able to praise a young Californian female impersonator as a great talent who ought to be in a New York review.

By the time that Isherwood arrived there, California was widely accepted as a haven for homosexuals from all over America. Isherwood, too, felt a new sense of personal freedom that had been impossible to achieve, even in Berlin. He wrote of himself in *Christopher and His Kind* 'his obligations wouldn't be the same in the States. He wouldn't be a member of a group. He could express himself freely as an individual.'

No longer driven by the embarrassment that had blighted his previous behaviour as a homosexual he abandoned all political causes and lived simply for himself and from February 1943 to August 1945, resided at the Vedanta Society in Hollywood studying to become a monk. Although he decided not to follow that vocation, he remained close to the Swami and continued to practice meditation. Isherwood had come a long way from the cynicism of his early days in Berlin but his sexuality remained as compulsive as ever. Much of his personal life continued to revolve around a sequence of younger lovers to whom he was a protective presence in his own laid-back version of Greek Love. One relationship in particular came to dominate his later life – Don Bachardy was 30 years his junior and became his partner and amanuensis for the rest of his life. Isherwood's post-war novels – *Prater Violet*, a satire on the movie business and *A Single Man* about the emergent gay movement – are a tribute to his singular talent. He died at home in southern California in 1986, almost 50 years after he had first arrived, having never once seriously considered ending his exile.

While Isherwood was drifting towards Hindu-inspired mysticism, W. H. Auden was making his own spiritual pilgrimage in the opposite direction. Preferring the intellectual rigour of New York to the individualism of California, he decided in 1940 to become a member of the Episcopal Church. This was the American equivalent of the Church of England that he had abandoned in his youth. His decision was greatly influenced by meeting Charles Williams, a novelist and committed Christian, who had also impressed the writers T. S. Eliot and C. S. Lewis.

Auden spent much of the war teaching in various American universities, but in the summer of 1945 he took a post as an observer of war damage and went to Germany with the US Strategic Bombing Survey. Seeing the city where he had spent the wild years of his youth in such total ruin was a shattering experience and this deeply affected his work. Auden became a naturalized US citizen in 1946, although he visited Europe every summer, starting in 1948. He was made a member of the American Academy and then Professor of Poetry at Oxford in 1955 where he was required to give three lectures each year. This fairly light workload allowed him to continue to winter in New York and to summer in Europe. In 1951, shortly before the two British spies Guy Burgess and Donald Maclean fled to the USSR, Burgess tried to call Auden to arrange a vacation visit to Ischia that he had discussed with him earlier. Although Auden never returned the call, the event was controversial and the British media was not slow to remind its readers of Auden's previous 'traitorous' action in abandoning his country for America in 1939. However, Auden's reputation as a writer had been largely restored and his decision to live almost his entire adult life in exile was forgiven if not totally forgotten. The legacy of his poems would in the end be seen as far more important than a self-serving and unpatriotic life.

PAUL BOWLES
AND GAY TANGIER

By 1945 war-torn Berlin was no longer the centre of European decadence it had been and many of the bars where Auden and Isherwood had picked up boys had been reduced to rubble. Instead, the Moroccan city of Tangier became the gay Mecca for a new generation of American and European exiles.

The main attraction of Morocco and the International Zone of Tangier, in particular, was that homosexuality was legal there. For decades its boy-brothels had made Tangier one of the most celebrated gay resorts in the world, although it lacked the cultural attractions of Paris or Berlin. Most importantly, it had the great advantage of being unusually safe for visitors as crime remained petty and homophobia was virtually unknown. Rather than being condemned as immoral infidels, the foreign homosexuals who arrived in the city were welcomed as a useful source of revenue.

Such visitors generally came from wealthy and privileged backgrounds and from countries where gay activities were still a criminal offence. In Britain, for example, active homosexuality was to remain illegal until 1967 when the *Sexual Offences Bill* was narrowly passed by Parliament. This act largely implemented the Wolfenden Committee's recommendation of a decade earlier that homosexual acts between consenting adults over the age of 21 should be decriminalized. The only exception was that no act should take place in public accommodation such as hotels or in a private home where a third person was likely to be present. What the new law finally established was that private morality or immorality was no longer the business of the state. The Wolfenden Report also directly influenced the American Bar Association's *Model Penal Code*, which set out to repeal sodomy laws and was adopted first by the state of Illinois in 1961. Pockets of resistance remained and even today some US states retain strict anti-sodomy laws. In 1945, however, none of this progressive legislation had taken place and in terms of tolerance little had changed since the 19th century anywhere other than in Italy, which was still recovering from the devastation of the war.

North Africa had long been associated with homoerotic activity. In the 1830s Algeria attracted many French gays only to be followed a century later by Morocco, where the International Zone that existed between 1923 and 1956 allowed a virtual *carte blanche* in sexual behaviour as it did for drug trafficking. Drawn by André Gide's romantic accounts of gay life in an exotic setting, those who went to Tangier or Marrakesh were sometimes disappointed by the sexual ambiguity they found there. Unlike the foreign visitors, many of the local men who appeared gay were actually married although they were bisexual and quite willing to participate in all-male sexual activity in return for financial reward or merely as a gesture of friendship. The sexual tourist was also faced with the moral dilemma that he was using his foreign money to exploit the misery of the poor locals. Conditions in many of the boy-brothels were appalling with orphans operating in windowless cells with primitive sanitation and scarcely space for a small bed.

This was the city, a place of squalor and excitement, that attracted the American writer and composer Paul Bowles (1910–99) and his bisexual wife Jane (1917–73) in September 1947. After war-torn Europe, Tangier appeared a charmed place and Paul Bowles was hooked from the start. He once explained his fascination for the place by saying:

> *Like any Romantic I had always been vaguely certain that sometime during my life I should come into a magic place which in disclosing its secrets would give me wisdom and ecstasy – perhaps even death.*

The magic of Tangier was to keep Bowles there for the next 52 years.

What attracted Bowles most was not just the sexual freedom but the realization that it was the place – cut off from the inhibitions and traditions of American and European culture – for him to develop as a writer. His staid background may explain his need for such an exotic location in adult life. Bowles was the son of a New York dentist who showed him little warmth while requiring the boy to conform to middle-class American behaviour. Bowles became particularly close to his gay Uncle Billy and while staying with him one evening found him dancing with another man in a close embrace. His uncle's anger at his nephew's presence shocked the boy who even at that age had developed an unusually cool and dispassionate attitude to sexual matters. This capacity for cold-eyed objectivity where love was concerned became a Bowles characteristic and reveals itself in his most explicitly homosexual story, *Pages from Cold Point*, about a boy who sets out to seduce his own father.

This lack of emotion may be attributed in part to Bowles's own sense of loneliness as a child, for he had few friends in New York and even when a student at the University of Virginia he failed to mix with others. Not surprisingly, he came to the conclusion that there was very little in American society to interest him and in the footsteps of Henry James, T. S. Eliot, Ernest Hemingway, Scott Fitzgerald and Gertrude Stein before him, he joined the steady stream of American artists and intellectuals who left for exile in Europe. Bowles wrote in his autobiography:

> *Everyone wanted to come to Europe in those days ... it was the intellectual and artistic centre. Paris specifically seemed to be the centre ... After all, it was the end of the twenties and just about everyone was in Paris.*

Bowles arrived in Paris in the summer of 1929 and found a job working on the switchboard of the *International Herald Tribune*. While in Paris he was at the centre of intellectual and creative life and was on friendly terms with Jean Cocteau (1889–1963), André Gide and Ezra Pound. On a visit to Berlin he met Christopher

Isherwood and the poet Stephen Spender (1909–95) and his own name may have inspired Isherwood to give the heroine of *Goodbye to Berlin* the name Sally Bowles.

At first Bowles concentrated on his music and took composition lessons from fellow American composers Virgil Thomson (1896–1989) and Aaron Copland (1900–90), who soon became his lover. Bowles claimed that Copland seduced him on their first night out together and that he had hated the experience, vowing that he would never again allow himself to be treated in this manner. What annoyed him was not the sex but the fact that Copland was his teacher and should not have compromised the master-teacher relationship. Yet Bowles learned a great deal from Copland and the result was a series of avant-garde operas, ballets, song cycles and orchestral pieces that he composed over the next two years. As promising as a musical career appeared, Bowles told friends that he could still not decide between being a composer or a writer. This indecision clouded his sex life as well, made even more confusing by a sexual encounter with his Uncle Billy who visited Paris. What little prose or poetry Bowles did write in Paris failed to satisfy him and when Gertrude Stein told him that she thought him 'not a real poet,' he reluctantly agreed.

Regardless of the stimulating company he enjoyed in Paris, the city failed to satisfy Bowles' creative need for somewhere more inspirational. When in August 1931 Gertrude Stein suggested that he try Tangier, where rents were cheap and pianos could be had for practically nothing, Bowles readily agreed.

Accompanied by Aaron Copland, Bowles sailed for Morocco the following month and later recalled his emotions as he saw 'the rugged line of the mountains of Algeria ahead and felt a great excitement'. Bowles was experiencing a landscape that had changed little in over a century. Both Eugène Delacroix (1798–1863) and Henri Matisse (1869–1954) had painted it, entranced by its unique combination of light and colour.

Arriving in the city he took a villa with Aaron Copland in the area known as the Old Mountain overlooking Tangier Bay. From that moment Bowles knew in his heart that he had found his own spiritual nirvana. In her book, *The Dream at the End of the World: Paul Bowles and the Literary Renegades in Tangier*, historian Michelle Green has summed up why the city at this time exercised such a strong appeal:

> *To expatriates who landed there after World War II, the International Zone of Tangier was an enigmatic, exotic and deliciously depraved version of Eden. A sun-beached, sybaritic outpost set against the verdant hills of North Africa, it offered a free money market and a moral climate in which only murder and rape were forbidden. Fleeing an angst-ridden Western culture, European émigrés found a haven where homosexuality was accepted, drugs were readily available and eccentricity was a social asset.*

Bowles felt immediately at home and his identification with the city became so complete that he claimed whenever he was away from Tangier, even for a few days, he began to miss the place. 'When I travel', he confessed to a friend, 'I get homesick for Tangier.' The city's unique status as an International Zone was the result of a territorial dispute between France and Spain that was resolved in 1923 by both countries agreeing to make the area around Tangier internationally neutrality, under the joint administration of both countries. As Bowles described it:

> *Morocco was still colonial, it was a place where any European could have anything. You could do anything because you ran it. Americans used to go up to the police and take hold of them and slap them in the face. The police couldn't do anything about it.*

This singular arrangement continued almost until Morocco's independence in 1956. Commercially, Tangier was an international freeport without the regulations and rigid customs duties of the rest of Europe, whereas socially it was a melting pot where people of all races met with the freedom to indulge in all forms of hedonistic behaviour, as long as they did not offend or insult Islam. Apart from the wide selection of drugs available, including kif – the local strain of African marijuana – there were possibilities for sexual encounters of every kind.

In many ways Tangier was a recreation of the Capri of the previous century and Bowles took to its pleasures with delight, using the city as the background for his novel *Let It Come Down* (1952). He claimed that without Tangier he might not have become a writer, once telling an interviewer 'probably if I hadn't had some contact with what you call "exotic" places, it couldn't have occurred to me to write at all.' His love affair with Tangier was to prove unshakeable throughout the following years, although he did return to the United States when the prospect of a European war became inevitable.

While in the New York apartment of the poet E.E. Cummings (1894–1962) in 1937, Bowles met the writer Jane Sidney Auer (1917–73). A confirmed lesbian, Auer was in poor physical shape suffering from tuberculosis of the leg bone. Close to despair she had decided that, in spite of her sexual orientation, she needed a man to look after her. Bowles, when propositioned, was intrigued by the prospect and promptly accepted, inviting Auer to head South with him. They travelled to Mexico and got married, forming a lasting relationship, although after little more than a year of heterosexuality they both agreed to go their own sexual ways. Their complicated relationship is reflected in one of Bowles's best-known novels *The Sheltering Sky* (1949).

Bowles had no objections to his wife sleeping with other women, such as the beautiful torch singer Libby Holman (1904–71), although Bowles later admitted that he would have been very jealous if Holman had been a man. Jane Bowles continued to have a series of female lovers many of them picked up in the lesbian and gay bars of Greenwich Village which she visited whenever she went back to New York. Her strangest relationship was with the great love of her life, a Moroccan woman named Cherifa, who was despised and feared by everyone in the Bowles' circle. After suffering a series of strokes which began when she was 40, Jane eventually became insane and died in a Malaga hospital in 1973; some of her friends believed that Cherifa had poisoned her.

Paul Bowles alternated between periods of celibacy and casual homosexual encounters with some of most famous creative talents of the age, including fellow American writers Tennessee Williams (1911–83) and Truman Capote (1924–84). Having returned to Tangier in 1947, Bowles remained there for the next 50 years. Curiously little had changed in Morocco since the 1930s in contrast to the other former colonial territories of North Africa. These more radical countries – Algeria, Tunisia and Libya – had gained their freedom after the Second World War (1939–45) and began discouraging homosexuality, seeing it as an unwelcome legacy of foreign rule. However, the tradition of gay travel once enjoyed by the likes of William Beckford (*see pages 49–60*) and Lord Byron (*see pages 69–78*) continued discreetly in Tangier long after independence. One chronicler of expatriate gay life in Tangier was the writer Robin Maugham (1916–81), nephew of novelist Somerset Maugham.

Many Americans also came to Tangier as life in their home country became increasingly puritanical. As always, the rich followed the intellectuals and Barbara Hutton (1912–79), the Woolworth heiress, bought a house in the Casbah, where she threw lavish parties. Her hospitality was only rivalled by that of the aristocratic Englishman David Herbert, son of the Earl of Pembroke, who moved to the city and became a close friend of the Bowles. Apart from his daily siesta, the fastidious Herbert hated being alone and encouraged his fellow 'Tangerines' to meet at lunchtimes on his terrace where a ready supply of food and drink awaited them. New faces from England earned a particularly warm welcome and especially anyone connected with literature or the arts. These same newcomers often gravitated to the Bowles's house where they found a man happy to have escaped middle-class America but wary of over-romanticizing the exoticism of Tangier. This mild conservatism occasionally put him at odds with the many hippies who flocked to the city throughout the late 1960s.

Earlier in the 1950s Paul Bowles had been the local patron saint of the Beats, a group of American writers who, like himself, rejected mainstream values. The leading members – Jack Kerouac (1922–69), Allen Ginsberg (1926–97) and William Burroughs (1914–97) – had arrived in Tangier to share Bowles's own experience of the exotic. Their stated intention was to deconstruct the existing social order by fracturing the shackles imposed by language itself. They questioned the nature of conventional perception by trying to make the experiences of dreams as valid as normal consciousness.

While Bowles was an inspirational force to the Beats, in reality his relationship to the movement was little more than that of Manet to the Impressionists. The loner Bowles always insisted that he could never be part of the Beats, although he felt a great deal of sympathy for their ideals. Where he differed most was in his unshakeable commitment to traditional craftsmanship in his writing, while their approach was far more casual and experimental. William Burroughs was typical of their random, unstructured method. He arrived in Tangier in 1954 on the run after shooting his wife dead during a drug-fuelled rage in Mexico. Hearing that he had arrived in Tangier, Bowles went in search of him and found the bisexual Burroughs lying on a bed in a cheap hotel room trying to kick his heroin addiction and repeatedly firing a pistol at the wall. Burroughs's decision to find exile in Tangier proved crucial for the writer and it spurred him to begin his novel *The Naked Lunch*. When Bowles arrived at his hotel one day with Brion Gysin (1916–86), another expatriate homosexual artist, he found Burroughs passed out on his bed and surrounded by the tatty manuscript of *The Naked Lunch*. Recognizing the potential of the work, they passed the text onto Kerouac and Ginsberg who agreed that it should be rescued and published. Bowles persuaded Burroughs to use a cut-and-paste technique of rearranging his text at random. The system proved a breakthrough for Burroughs, encouraging the full release of his creative drive and he rapidly composed new random passages full of mysticism and hidden meaning. When the innovative book was published by Olympia Press in Paris in 1959 it was immediately recognized as a landmark of modern American literature.

Bowles continued to enjoy the pleasures of Tangier life, even after Moroccan independence in 1956 and Tangier's reintegration with Morocco under the Tangier Protocol of October 1956, and the low cost of living meant that he had few financial problems. Most of the pleasures, however, were completely free, such as the sights and sounds of the exotic city. What intrigued him most as a composer was the strange and primitive Moroccan music that could constantly be heard drifting up to his house. Most nights the drumming in the city infiltrated his dreams along with the cries of the muezzins calling people to prayer. These experiences fired his interest in the music of the Moroccan Berbers and he passed on his enthusiasm not only to Burroughs and Ginsberg but also to a younger generation of visiting rock stars, such as the Rolling Stones, David Bowie (b.1947) and Paul McCartney (b.1942).

Although romantically attached to North Africa, Bowles could never fully immerse himself in its culture. He remained a sympathetic outsider whose cultural roots remained firmly anchored in the Western European tradition of literature and music. By keeping his head, if not his heart, firmly in the Western cultural tradition, Bowles provided an important and influential link for those artists intrigued by North African culture. His presence in Tangier continued to attract other gay writers including Gore Vidal (b.1925) and British playwright Joe Orton (1933-67), and also the painter Francis Bacon (1909-92).

Bowles's own work explored aspects of drugs and sexuality that pioneered new artistic freedom as Norman Mailer wrote of him:

> *Paul Bowles opened the world of Hip. He let in the murder, the drugs, the incest, the death of the Square, the call of the orgy, the end of civilization.*

By the 1960s, the appeal of Tangier as a gay refuge was diminishing as San Francisco began to draw those who would once have thought of heading for North Africa. Yet, Tangier remained Paul Bowles's home until his death there in 1999.

Indeed, the atmosphere of sexual tolerance in Tangier continued into the 1980s before fundamentalist Islamic thinking gained dominance in Moroccan society, bringing with it a steadily increasing reaction against Western tourism and the moral degeneracy associated with it.

JAMES BALDWIN'S RETREAT TO FRANCE

None of the wealthy white gay men drawn to Tangier in the post-war period experienced any of the early problems that faced black writer James Baldwin (1924–87). They may have despised the materialism of America but they depended on its wealth to finance their exile in Morocco. Baldwin came from a completely different background marked by deprivation and racial oppression. Yet, he shared with Henry James his ambition to become a great writer and recognized, like the white patrician writer, that he could only achieve that ambition by exiling himself from his homeland. James once observed that it was a complex fate to be an American and that the principle discovery that an American writer makes in Europe is to realize just how complex this fate is. For Baldwin being small, black, odd-looking and openly gay were additional burdens for his voyage to self-discovery. He later wrote of his decision to live in exile in France: 'I wanted to find in what way the specialness of my experience could be made to connect me with other people, instead of dividing me from them.'

James Baldwin was born in Harlem, New York, to a single mother in August 1924. While he was still a small child, his mother married David Baldwin, an itinerant preacher from Louisiana, who made the young boy's childhood a misery. Ignoring James's obvious intelligence, his stepfather preferred to mock his ugliness, claiming that it was the mark of the devil. Throughout his life Baldwin constantly related an incident involving his looks which he claimed changed his life. When he was about six years old, he went to the window and saw on the street an old woman with large bulbous eyes and thick swollen lips. He ran upstairs, called his mother to the window saying 'You see? You see? She's uglier than you, Mama! She's uglier than me!' Several years later the true meaning of the experience came to him when he realized that his physical appearance was irrelevant to his purpose in life and 'that if my mother was ugly then even ugliness could be beautiful'. The ordeal that he suffered at his stepfather's hands was used as material for his first novel *Go Tell It on the Mountain*, written in 1953. The novel examines the role of the Church in the lives of African Americans as a source of repression and hypocrisy while at the same time recognizing that it sustains an oppressed people. Like Baldwin, the young protagonist in the book struggles with his homosexual leanings and this aspect of the work saw it banned in several American states.

In reality Baldwin was living through what must have been a living hell for a sensitive man constantly abused and treated badly by black and white alike. As a teenager he found himself the victim of police discrimination and attacks from his black neighbours led him to turn in desperation to the Church. His sense of confusion was so profound that when a black woman preacher, Mother Horn, asked him rhetorically whose little boy he was Baldwin simply answered 'Why, yours' and immediately joined her church. Surprisingly given the abuse he had earlier suffered, Baldwin then began attending services at his stepfather's Pentecostal church before becoming a junior minister himself. The weekly sermons full of evangelical emotion and dramatic warnings of heaven and hell were a useful introduction to the imagery that he later used in his novels. Like many other young people, he was living through a period of self-imposed Puritanism that involved reading the Bible and total abstinence from such simple pleasures as going to the movies. The black lesbian writer Azaan Kamau, who grew up in the same society as Baldwin, has written that black homosexuals were caught in the middle of a society fuelled by religion and facing irrational hatred. In many cases all that they had to draw on was their own religious faith and as a result their beliefs were often based on destructive interpretations of the Bible. Often their own people were their greatest critics and they misinterpreted information taken from the Bible to ostracize the lesbians and homosexuals in their community.

This uncharacteristic period of religious piety was short lived and by the time he graduated from college in 1942, James Baldwin had abandoned church and adopted a more open-minded attitude to life. The bitterness he felt was far more difficult to shake off and his anger was reignited when during the war he sought work in a New Jersey armaments factory. There, he soon learned that all the bars, bowling alleys, diners and decent apartments were closed to black Americans. A dogged determination born out of the suffering he had already endured now surfaced and, long before the Civil Rights Movement of the 1960s, Baldwin staged his own one-man protest. If a bar or restaurant displayed a notice barring blacks he would deliberately go in and sit down thus forcing the staff to refuse to serve him. He once described his last night in New Jersey when having been refused service in a diner, he went into 'an enormous, glittering and fashionable restaurant in which I knew not even the intercession of the Virgin would cause me to be served'. He sat at a table until a waitress came and predictably told him 'We don't serve Negroes here.' He noted the fear and the apology in her voice but still 'I wanted her to come close enough for me to get her neck between my hands.' Instead, he threw a half-full mug of water at her that missed and then ran out of the restaurant.

Later, Baldwin realized that he had been ready to commit murder that night and that 'my life, my real life, was in danger, and not from anything other people might do but from the hatred I carried in my own heart.' He felt this impotent rage must be known to every black American. His experience of working-class life in the factory and briefly at a construction company in New Jersey convinced Baldwin that he must escape the limitations of American society and its banal concept of masculinity in which:

> ... the ideal had created cowboys and Indians, good guys and bad guys, tough guys and softies, butch and faggot, black and white. It is an ideal so paralytically infantile that it is virtually forbidden – an unpatriotic act – that the American boy evolve into the complexity of manhood.

Now Baldwin was fully committed to becoming a writer and moved to New York where he took a room in Greenwich Village, the creative centre of the city and supposedly the least racially prejudiced part of the country. Here he set about learning his craft as a novelist and produced his first two works·*Crying Holy* and *In My Father's House*, before completing the far more ambitious *Go Tell It on the Mountain*.

Life in Greenwich Village proved a disappointment for even in this liberal place he still had to contend with the almost daily racial prejudice that he had known since childhood. The one compensation was that in New York he could more openly express his homosexuality and he began a series of short-lived and unsatisfying relationships with other men. These experiences only produced more confusion, causing Baldwin to re-examine his sexual orientation and come to the conclusion, albeit briefly, that he was not gay after all. The result was a relationship with a young woman that led to an engagement but finally Baldwin decided that to maintain his integrity and to develop as a writer he must leave the country. In November 1948, having just been awarded a Rosenwald Fellowship for African Americans, Baldwin bought a one-way ticket to France. One of his last acts before departure was to cancel his wedding plans and to throw both engagement rings into the Hudson River as a gesture of final severance with his conventional sexuality. He had realized that as a maverick he could not remain in the United States for he could depend on neither the white world nor the black worlds, 'I had to say, "A curse on both your houses." The fact that I went to Europe so early is probably what saved me. It gave me another touchstone - myself.' Baldwin decided that his revenge for the indignities that he had suffered in America would be to become a great writer like Henry James and 'to achieve a power that outlasts kingdoms'.

Within a few months of arriving in France, Baldwin was able to put his life into perspectiv. He later told the *New York Times*:

> *Once I found myself on the other side of the ocean. I could see where I came from very clearly, and I could see that I carried*

myself, which is my home, with me. You can never escape
that. I am the grandson of a slave, and I am a writer. I must
deal with both.

His move to Paris had been encouraged by his gay friend, the black
artist Beauford Delaney (1901–79), who was already living there.
Delaney became a father figure to Baldwin and helped him settle
into his new home. Increasingly, however, Delaney began to show
signs of mental instability and his eventual confinement in a
mental hospital caused his younger friend much distress.

For a man coming from the most celebrated new democracy of
the modern world it was Europe's traditional society that most
appealed to Baldwin. He was impressed that a writer was respected
in France for what he did, in the same way that a good baker or a
skilled craftsman were. This was so different to the country he had
left, where commercial success was prized above creative talent. In
the years that followed Baldwin lived as he had never been able to
do in New York. He moved from the Right Bank to the Left; he
mixed with the bourgeoisie and the poor, with intellectuals and
with pimps, with the prostitutes of Pigalle and with the wealthy
bankers of Neuilly. The irony was that in what was supposedly a
class-ridden European society, he was more at ease and able to talk
to more people from different backgrounds than he had ever been
in the so-called open democracy of the United States. This
realization came as a profound shock and resulted in a mental
breakdown. He retreated to the Swiss mountains to convalesce and
there, armed with just two Bessie Smith records and a typewriter,
he reassessed his past life and prepared for the future in what was
almost a form of spiritual rebirth. As he wrote at the time ,what he
had really learned by his French exile 'was about my own country,
my own past, and about my own language.' As James Joyce had
been able to bring Dublin life into focus by his exile in Trieste so
Baldwin was now able, at a distance to write more passionately
about America.

There was one legacy, however, that refused to go away, that of
racial tension. Even in France he found that black Americans were
often viewed, particularly by their visiting white countrymen, with

the same hostility that greeted the Algerian Arabs. There was also another racial complication that was new to him, the obvious tension between 'brown' African Americans and the 'black' African immigrants. Baldwin experienced police hostility when he was arrested for inadvertently accepting a stolen bed sheet from a friend. Locked in a cell without shoelaces or belt and treated with contempt as a black person, he realized that racism was not confined to the United States. Over the coming years his experience in that French cell helped galvanize his efforts to support the Civil Rights Movement and in many of his essays, novels, plays and speeches, he used his natural eloquence to support the struggle for black Americans. His views on the issue can be seen as a fusion of the two leading protagonists, Malcolm X (1925–65) and Martin Luther King, Jr (1929–68), but as he said himself 'I was a maverick, a maverick in the sense that I depended on neither the white world nor the black world.'

What was so original about Baldwin compared to other black activists of the time was that he thought racism was a white rather than a black problem. White society had to come to terms with its own history of oppression and realize that it could no longer exercise dominance – compassion and a new sense of community were essential for everyone's survival.

Such views meant that James Baldwin was largely rejected by both extremes of the Civil Rights Movement. To the followers of the moderate Martin Luther King, Jr, he was seen as a radical and for this reason was not asked to speak at the March on Washington in August 1963, even though he was the most distinguished black American writer of the time. To the militants led by Malcolm X, Bobby Seale (b.1936) and Huey Newton (1942–89), Baldwin was far too passive in his approach. His greatest critic was Eldridge Cleaver (1935–98), a spokesman for the Black Panthers who attacked Baldwin for pandering to white society as a writer and for selling out his black manhood by being openly gay. Yet, Cleaver must have known that his colleague Malcolm X, the leader of the Nation of Islam and the best known of all the black activists, had had homosexual experiences himself. In a series of candid interviews Malcolm X revealed to his biographer Bruce Perry, that he was not the tough, no-nonsense heterosexual that everyone supposed. From the age of 20 he had sex with men for money and he had at least one sustained sexual liaison with a man. There were witnesses to this; his room-mate while he was living in Flint, Michigan, noticed that instead of sleeping in the room they were sharing, Malcolm often sneaked down the hall to spend the night with a gay transvestite named Willie Mae.

In spite of the pressure to conform to one or other faction, James Baldwin remained his own man, firm in his belief that the struggle was not really about black rights or even civil rights but about human rights. He believed that the Civil Rights Movement should be just one part of a universal crusade that sought the freedom of people everywhere. This concern with events in America did not prevent Baldwin enjoying the life of an increasingly successful writer in France. His biographer and one-time secretary, David Leeming, portrayed Baldwin as an indefatigable partygoer capable of consuming vast amounts of liquor at a sitting. Often these excesses provoked errors of judgement that led Baldwin into highly compromising sexual situations. Soon after his arrival in Paris Baldwin fell in love with a 17-year-old runaway, Lucien Happsberger, whose marriage three years later completely devastated Baldwin. Baldwin was constantly drawn to heterosexual men. Often after the end of such an affair, Baldwin would sink into a profound depression, during which he would talk of suicide and on several occasions might have carried out his threats if friends had not intervened.

Whether in high or low spirits, Baldwin continued to write unceasingly, honing his skill as a novelist and producing a whole stream of creative work, including his most famous novel about gay life, *Giovanni's Room*. This was not his first attempt to deal with homosexuality: as early as 1949 he had an essay on the subject published in an obscure Moroccan journal. Such were the times that it was not published in America until 1989. One of the few pieces of non-fiction that Baldwin ever wrote, it defends the naturalness and legitimacy of homosexual desire and suggests that homophobia is the direct result of heterosexual anxiety. The resulting hostility towards gays, like that against blacks, indicates a complete failure of imagination and a dangerous inability to acknowledge one's own innate humanity. Two years later, in 1951, Baldwin returned to the theme, this time in his first fiction, a short story entitled *Outing*. The theme is the sexual awakening of two adolescent boys who spend a day together on a church picnic and one begins to realize his powerful sexual feelings for the other.

Except for the occasional trip back to the US, Baldwin was to remain in France for the rest of his life, although he frequently visited rural Switzerland and Istanbul. During his time in Paris and later at his home in St Paul de Vence in Provence he published 22 books during a career that lasted nearly 40 years.

Although France had become his home and life there suited his temperament, he never gave up his American citizenship. He once commented that he preferred to think of himself as a commuter between the two countries rather than an expatriate. He believed that only white Americans could consider themselves expatriates; for himself it was only when he had left his homeland that he could really see where he came from. What he found in Paris was a sense of territorial and personal freedom that he had never experienced in New York. Certainly, the French were pleased to have such a distinguished writer as one of their own and recognized his contribution to the cultural life of the nation by awarding him in 1986 the Commandership of the Legion of Honour.

James Baldwin's journey from a difficult childhood in Harlem to his eventual status as a legendary artist with a large and loyal international audience constitutes one of the most compelling American biographies of the 20th century. Perhaps the most touching tribute to Baldwin came from the *Washington Post* columnist Juan Williams, who concluded:

> *The success of Baldwin's effort as the witness is evidenced time and again by the people, black and white, gay and straight, famous and anonymous, whose humanity he unveiled in his writings. America and the literary world are far richer for his witness.*

THE END OF EXILE

Today, in the West at least, homosexuals are no longer persecuted or driven into exile and tolerance is enshrined in the laws of most democracies. Yet the ascendancy of Islamic fundamentalism in parts of the Middle East, Africa and South-East Asia has ushered in a new era of religious intolerance and homophobia. The liberal and compassionate wing of Islam is being increasingly suppressed by a rigorous and violent interpretation of the Koran. The fervour of this modern Muslim extremism against gays is a grim echo of the homophobia of Europe that drove men such as Théophile de Viau and William Beckford into exile centuries ago. Same-sex relationships are currently outlawed in no less than 26 Islamic countries ranging from Afghanistan to the Yemen. Active persecution of gays varies from country to country but the Islamic Republic of Iran is the most vigorous in punishing homosexuals and it has executed 4,000 lesbians and gay men since Ayatollah Khomeini (1902–89) rose to power in 1979. Indeed, the death toll over the 10-year period of Khomeini's rule accounts for far more than those killed by the Holy Inquisition in Europe at the height of its power.

Iran makes no secret of its campaign against same-sex relationships and those who can, escape into exile – all those who remain are at risk of suffering the most brutal punishments. The situation is similar to that once faced by homosexuals in Nazi Germany where denouncement to the authorities for whatever motive would result in imprisonment or death. Again, as under Hitler's regime, the government is immune to international criticism. In September 2007, the Iranian President Mahmoud Ahmadinejad (b.1956) made his notorious claim at Columbia

University that in Iran, 'we do not have homosexuals like in your country'. The absurdity of the claim was recognized by the whole of the non-Islamic world. The feminist writer and researcher Janet Afary has shown through close examination of ancient texts that same-sex relationships have been a characteristic of Iranian society throughout history, particularly in the Persian form of Greek Love in which an older man tutors and protects a younger. As in 4th-century Athens, these activities were regulated by recognized rules of behaviour and courtship that included the giving of presents, studying and taking part in sport and military training. Just as intriguing was the discovery that these same-sex relationships existed among Persian women too and had even persisted into the 20th century. A long courtship was customary with the women exchanging gifts and travelling together to religious shrines where they occasionally spent the night together. These courtship rituals were governed by custom and any woman who sought a 'sister' would use a love broker. In the court of Naser al-Din Shah, who ruled Persia throughout the second half of the 19th century, keeping boy-concubines was still common practice and the Shah in addition to his many wives and full harem kept a boy himself. Perhaps surprisingly, such traditions were still common in the early 20th century, as Iranian society continued to accept both male and female homoerotic practices. All this ended when the fundamentalists came to power as can be seen by the fate of one Iranian lesbian who escaped to exile in Britain in 2005. Arrested and tortured for the first time when she was 21, the woman spent three months in prison. Refusing to conform she was then imprisoned for two years, given 160 lashes and threatened with death by hanging or burning if she repeated the offence again.

The first sign of the rise of homophobia in Iran appeared at the time of the First World War in an Azeri-language newspaper called *Molla Nasreddin* that became the mouthpiece of the new Iranian Revolution movement. As much opposed to traditional sexual freedom as it was to the autocracy of the regime, the newspaper shared Karl Marx's well-known contempt for gay people. The newspaper began attacking gays as corrupting paedophiles and clerical teachers in particular were declared to be molesters of innocent young boys. Cleverly the argument linked those members of the ruling elite that it wished to overthrow with such practices as keeping young men as amrad or concubines. This suggestion that political corruption was inseparable from sexual deviance became a popular theme for an increasing number of radical Iranian journals in which leading members of the political establishment were attacked for their supposed homosexuality. Leading this homophobic crusade was the journalist Ahmad Kasravi (1890–1946), founder of the nationalist movement, Pak Dini or Purity of Religion. Kasravi was largely responsible for formulating many of the cultural and educational policies that would later characterize modern Iran. Interestingly, he came up with a novel criticism of homosexuality claiming that it was a sign of cultural backwardness in a society and that the Sufi poets who had praised homoeroticism were no more than parasites and their work should be destroyed. At Kasravi's instigation Pak Dini members set about burning the books in the manner of Savonarola's Bonfire of the Vanities and Goebbels's conflagration of the works of Jewish and 'degenerate' authors in Berlin.

Eventually the Iranian Revolution triumphed and the old regime under the Shah and the liberal, if corrupt, elite was overthrown. With the return of Ayatollah Khomeini in February 1979 religious law was steadily imposed on the nation. The death penalty was soon applied not only for sodomy but also for repeated offences of lesser sexual acts such as mutual masturbation and 'body rubbing'. The mere act of two people of the same sex lying naked together without just cause became a crime punishable by up to 99 lashes. One man kissing another, even without lust, earned 60 lashes. In 1990 the Iranian crusade against homosexuality was highlighted by a wave of public executions that commenced with three men savagely beheaded in a city square in Nahavand and two women accused of lesbianism being stoned to death in Langrood. Justifying these killings, the Iranian Chief Justice, Morteza Moghtadai, declared that 'the religious punishment for the despicable act of homosexuality is death for both parties'. His colleague Ayatollah Ali Khamenei (b. 1939) then condemned Britain and the US for promoting gay relationships claiming that the two countries had insulted God by legalizing marriages between people of the same sex. Ayatollah Musavi-Ardebili went even further, demanding the strict enforcement of Islamic punishments which he described to the students at Tehran University in blood-curdling detail:

> *They should seize him or her, they should keep him standing, they should split him in two with a sword, they should either cut off his neck or they should split him from the head ... after he is dead, they bring logs, make a fire and place the corpse on the logs, set fire to it and burn it. Or it should be taken to the top of a mountain and thrown down. Then the parts of the corpse should be gathered together and burnt. Or they should dig a hole, make a fire in the hole and throw him alive into the fire ... there cannot be the slightest degree of mercy or compassion.... Praise be to God.*

These words with their obsession with fire and burning could easily have been written by the Christian St Peter Damian (1007–72) or any of the religious zealots of the Spanish Inquisition almost a millennium earlier. Today Iranian law continues to punish all penetrative sexual acts between adult men with the death penalty. Non-penetrative activities between men are punished with lashes until the fourth offence at which time death is mandatory. Sexual acts between women are also punished with lashes until the fourth offence when again the death penalty is imposed. Judges accept confessions produced under torture and those charged are regularly denied the assistance of lawyers. Iran also has its own version of England's 18th-century Society for the Reformation of Manners called the Special Protection Division. This state-controlled organization routinely uses informants on immoral behaviour in every town in the country. More recently Internet chat rooms have been used to locate members of the gay community. Once a suspect is identified a meeting is arranged and he or she is arrested by undercover agents and taken into custody where torture is used to extract a confession. When addressing a group of British MPs in 2007, the Iranian politician Mohsen Yahyavi stated quite openly that in the opinion of his government all homosexuals deserved to be tortured or executed or both.

The result of this police state is that every lesbian and gay in Iran lives in a state of almost complete isolation and panic, wary lest a school friend, an employer or even a hostile family member denounce them to the authorities. As a result many Iranian gays have sought to escape this society. As one who succeeded put it:

> I soon realized that I had to leave my home country. Even if I refrained from being an activist and never again submitted a single article to an underground newspaper, my life would be in constant jeopardy: at any moment a friend being tortured inside a prison could reveal my name. Arrest would not only end my life but also disgrace my entire family. And how many names would I reveal once they started beating me on the soles of my feet, or hanging me from iron bars?

This man joined the growing band of Iranian gay exiles attempting to find refuge in other countries. This has not been an easy task for in spite of the Iranian government's persecution many Western governments are still reluctant to give these gay exiles sanctuary. Even the traditionally liberal Netherland's government refused to stop deporting gay men back to Iran with the Dutch Immigration Minister claiming disingenuously that 'there is no question of executions or death sentences based solely on the fact that a defendant is gay.' After a public outcry in October 2006 the minister was forced to reverse his decision and announced that in future no Iranian gay exiles would be deported from the Netherlands.

Iran is not alone in actively persecuting homosexuals. In Saudi Arabia Filipino guest workers risk 200 lashes for any signs of gay behaviour while the native Saudis themselves live under strictly homophobic sharia law by which sodomy is punishable by death even though this extreme penalty is seldom applied.

Homosexuality is publicly condemned but as long as gays and lesbians appear to conform to normal Wahhabi behaviour, they are left to do what they want in private. The country has its own form of 'doublethink' for many of the men having sex with other men do not consider themselves gay at all and rather like the miners in the Californian Gold Rush, believe that they are merely fulfilling a desire or a temporary need and not expressing an identity. Nor does a man lose his masculinity in such an encounter as long as he plays the active role in sex.

At a time when homosexuality has become increasingly accepted in Europe it remains a divisive issue in Africa. In Uganda a coalition of Christian and Muslim religious groups united to call for the mass arrest and punishment of gay people. The government appeared sympathetic to this lobbying for so-called Ethics and Integrity Minister, James Nsaba Buturo, told a news conference in 2004 that he was concerned about what he called the 'mushrooming' number of gays and lesbians in the country and that planned legislation would soon criminalize gay behaviour. One of his keenest supporters was a well-known Muslim cleric, Sheikh Ramathan Shaban Mubajje, who proposed the simple expedient of shipping all of Uganda's gays and lesbians to an island in the middle of Lake Victoria and leaving them there in a tropical version of a Stalinist gulag.

That same year, President Sam Nujoma of Namibia proved that Christianity could be just an intolerant as Islam by telling his people that same-sex relationships are against God's will and warning them that 'the Republic of Namibia does not allow homosexuality or lesbianism here. Police are ordered to arrest you, deport you and imprison you.' His words were endorsed by the country's Home Affairs Minister, who urged newly graduated police officers to 'eliminate gays and lesbians from the face of Namibia.' The same homophobic sentiments have been voiced by other African leaders, including Robert Mugabe (b.1924; president of Zimbabwe since 1987) who, by focusing public attention on the supposed gay problem, has sought to divert attention from his own corrupt regime. Only one African country, the Republic of South

Africa, has refused to join this homophobic crusade. Instead it has become a world leader in civil rights for gays and lesbians and is the first country to adopt a constitution that comprehensively outlaws discrimination against homosexuals and lesbians.

While it is easy to criticize African leaders for using scare tactics against gay people for political ends it should not be forgotten that the US went down this dangerous path just over 50 years ago when Senator Joseph McCarthy (1908–57) used accusations of homosexuality as a smear tactic in his anti-communist crusade. This assumed connection between homosexuality and a lack of patriotism was exactly the same argument that was exploited by Hitler and Stalin in the 1930s. Some historians have argued that in linking Communism to homosexuality in his so-called 'Lavender Scare', McCarthy was exploiting prevalent anxieties about sexuality in order to gain support for his anti-communist campaign. He was enthusiastically supported in this by Senator Kenneth Wherry, who claimed that 'you can't separate homosexuals from subversives'. Wherry promoted the fiction that Josef Stalin had obtained from Hitler a list of closeted homosexuals in positions of power in the US who could be blackmailed to betray vital security information. Even the Under-Secretary of State at the time, James E. Webb, reported that 'It is generally believed that those who engage in overt acts of perversion lack the emotional stability of normal persons.' As a result of this homophobic and political witch-hunt between 1,700 federal job applications were denied, 4,380 people were discharged from the military and 420 were fired from their government jobs.

Public opinion on homosexuality has changed significantly since the McCarthy era with 57 percent of the American public now believing it to be an acceptable alternative lifestyle and a further 59 percent willing to see gay relationships recognised in law. The sexually open and tolerant society that men like A. J. Symonds and Edward Carpenter dreamed of is, at least in the West, now coming into being. The simple and indisputable truth that a person's sexuality is determined at birth and not the result of an act of will is now generally accepted. What has also helped change public opinion has been the attitude of gay people themselves as they have increasingly shown over the past few decades that they are no longer prepared to be harassed or bullied. The direct action of the Civil Rights Movement through its marches, demonstrations and protests showed that the gay community could successfully adopt a similar approach.

The most important single event in this process was the Stonewall Riots that began on 28 June 1969 at the Stonewall Inn, a popular gay bar in Greenwich Village, Exasperated by constant police raids, on this particular night the clientele decided to fight back and took to the streets in a spontaneous and violent demonstration. The tensions between New York City police and the gay residents of Greenwich Village erupted into more protests on subsequent nights. The Village residents then organized themselves into action groups that would defend other gay bars and meeting places.

This was the first instance in American history of gays and lesbians turning on their oppressors and fighting back. It was a defining moment that marked the beginning of the militant gay rights movement in the US and around the world. Three years later, the US Department of the Interior designated the site of the Stonewall Inn – 51 and 53 Christopher Street and the surrounding streets – a National Historic Landmark. In doing so it became the first historic reference to gays and lesbians since the statue to Harmodius and Aristogiton in ancient Athens. At the dedication ceremony, the assistant secretary of the Department of the Interior made the following enlightened statement:

> Let it forever be remembered that here – on this spot – men and women stood proud, they stood fast, so that we may be who we are, we may work where we will, live where we choose and love whom our hearts desire.

Of equal significance were the reforms that took place in the Soviet Union with the fall of Communism including the unexpected liberalization of gay life in Russia under the enlightened regime of Mikhail Gorbachev (b.1931; general secretary of the Communist

Party of the Soviet Union 1985–91 and president of the Soviet Union 1990–91) and the period of glasnost – a policy of open discussion of political and social issues that started the democratization of the Soviet Union.

One of the many momentous actions that marked the opening up of Russian life was the formation of the Moscow Gay and Lesbian Alliance and the many gay publications that began to appear in Russian bookshops. Such freedom of expression would have been unthinkable under previous regimes. In 1991 came the first international gay conference, film festival and open but peaceful demonstrations for gay rights on the streets of Moscow and Leningrad. This whole process appeared threatened when traditional hardliners staged an attempted coup against Boris Yeltsin (1931–2007; president of Russia 1990–2000) in August 1991. Had it succeeded there is little doubt that firm action would have been taken to suppress emerging gay and lesbian freedoms. Many gay activists manned the barricades protecting the Russian White House that day, to make sure that Yeltsin would survive and that the reactionaries were routed. The result was a new era of personal freedom that resulted two years later in a new Russian Criminal Code that no longer contained the infamous Article 121 criminalizing homosexual activity between men. Those already imprisoned under the old law were soon released and gay bars, discos and saunas began to flourish.

In recent centuries people sexually attracted to others of the same gender came to define themselves in terms of their sexuality. This creation of a gay identity had started in 18th-century Europe when migration to the cities and the need to band together to resist persecution brought about the conditions for the emergence of a gay culture. Prior to that, no one would think of describing themselves according to their sexual preferences because there were only homosexual acts, not homosexual people. The distinction between 'the homosexual' and 'the heterosexual' was therefore a novelty. Perhaps this time will come again when, as in the past, homosexuals did not exist and there were only people who had sex with others of the same gender. Perhaps in the future the word gay or homosexual will serve only to describe a form of behaviour and not a type of person. In other words, both 'the homosexual and 'the heterosexual' will cease to exist. Without these brandings there will be no justification for homophobia for without differentiation and separation there can be no conflict. Perhaps the last word on the subject should remain with Edward Carpenter, a courageous pioneer of openness in sexual matters, who more than 60 years before the modern gay liberation movement came into existence made a prophetic statement that he hoped would end gay exile forever:

The Uranian [gay] people may be destined to form the advance guard of that great movement which will one day transform the common life by substituting the bond of personal affection and compassion for the monetary, legal and other external ties which now control and confine society.

Yet, in spite of the suffering there have been positive aspects of gay exile for it often provoked a flowering of creativity that would have been impossible if the individual had remained in the conservative and inhibiting culture where he or she originated. Without self-imposed exile from America would Henry James, Paul Bowles or James Baldwin have been able to realize to the full their innate talents as writers? Had Queen Christina remained in Sweden could she have attained the personal and spiritual freedom that she found in Italy? And, without exile would W. H. Auden and Christopher Isherwood have been able to throw off the stultifying English hypocrisy that had earlier ruined the emotional lives of sensitive men such as Edward Lear?

Perhaps one of the most positive images of gay exile with which to leave you should that of the Ladies of Llangollen in their Welsh mountain retreat admired from afar and free to enjoy the love of each other with an intensity that few contemporary heterosexual relationships could ever ever achieved.

BIOGRAPHIES

Aristogiton and Harmodius (d.514BC)

Demonstrated the power of Greek Love by slaying the tyrant Hipparchus in the name of Athenian democracy. They were honoured as heroes.

Sappho (c.630-570BC)

The most famous lesbian of the Ancient world. Sappho founded a school of poetry on the Island of Lesbos. She was exiled to Sicily by the tyrant Pittacus.

Benvenuto Cellini (1500-71)

One of the great Italian goldsmiths and sculptors of the Renaissance. Cellini was imprisoned for his wild homosexual lifestyle, then went into self-imposed exile in France in 1537, before returning to Rome five years later.

Théophile de Viau (1590-1626)

French poet and Libertine who wrote of male love. He was exiled to England for homosexual behaviour in 1619, but returned to France in 1622. He became a cause célèbre in Europe after he was again imprisoned and sentenced to perpetual banishment.

Queen Christina of Sweden (1626-89)

Christina's masculine attitudes, cross-dressing and love for a female courtier caused little friction in Sweden. But her decision to abandon her country and her religion to live as a Catholic in Rome scandalized northern Europe.

Thomas Gray (1716-71)

English poet, who suppressed his strong homosexual tendencies by choosing the seclusion of university life, after a period of exile in Europe on the Grand Tour. Gray's homoerotic feelings led him to write some of the best poetry of the 18th century.

Horace Walpole (1717-97)

Aesthete and novelist. He shared the Grand Tour with Thomas Gray but was equally careful to avoid gay relationships for the rest of his life.

William Beckford (1760-1844)

Wealthiest man in England and author of the gothic novel *Vathek*. Beckford conducted a disastrous and indiscreet affair with his nephew, which led to his own disgrace and exile.

Ladies of Llangollen: Eleanor Butler (1739-1829) and Sarah Ponsonby (1755-1831)

Two Anglo-Irish gentlewomen, who ran away and found happiness together in exile in

Llangollen, North Wales. Their gentle lesbianism and idyllic lifestyle attracted many admirers in English society.

Anne Lister (1791–1840)

'The first modern lesbian.' Lister spent much of her time travelling in Europe with her lover and wrote one the most open and pioneering accounts of homosexuality.

Lord Byron (1788–1824)

The greatest romantic poet and bisexual of the age. Byron was driven into exile by English society because of homosexual revelations. He deeply admired the concept of Greek Love. Byron died in the cause of Greek freedom at Missalonghi.

Edward Lear (1812–88)

A fine artist and the most celebrated humorist of the 19th century, famous for his Nonsense verse. Lear was a victim of his own timidity in refusing either to marry or acknowledge his own homosexuality.

Baron Wilhelm von Gloeden (1856–1931)

A pioneering gay photographer who used Italian youths to recreate images of Ancient Greece. He lived in exile at Taormina, in Sicily, and helped to make it a destination for European and American homosexuals.

Count Jacques d'Adelswird Fersen (1880–1923)

A French writer who exiled himself from Paris following imprisonment and social disgrace due to a scandal involving young boys. He settled on the island of Capri and lived an openly homosexual lifestyle, thereby attracting those with similar feelings to the island.

Frederick Rolfe (1860–1913)

English writer, who was better known as Baron Corvo. Rolfe was a cantankerous but highly original writer obsessed with Roman Catholicism. He eventually exiled himself to Venice where his homosexuality was tolerated but he lived in constant financial difficulty.

A. J. Symonds (1840–93)

English poet and critic. Symonds struggled to conform within his heterosexual marriage. He came out and went into exile at Davos in Switzerland. Symonds was an early champion of openness in sexual matters and his memoirs are one of the first honest records of modern homosexuality.

Edward Carpenter (1844–1929)

Socialist, poet and early gay activist. Carpenter was a strong advocate of all forms of sexual freedom. His work inspired many others to be open about their homosexuality.

Oscar Wilde (1854–1900)

Great comic dramatist who refused to hide his homosexuality. His affair with Lord Alfred Douglas led to his imprisonment and subsequent exile in France. Wilde was the most famous victim of 19th century homophobia.

Henry James (1843-1916)

American novelist who spent much of his life in either Paris or London. James was careful to suppress his homosexual feelings and to devote himself entirely to his work.

E. M. Forster (1879-1970)

English novelist and member of the sexually radical Bloomsbury Set. Forster's attitude towards his homosexuality was ambiguous. He found sexual fulfilment with non-European men when abroad, living in Egypt or India.

Natalie Clifford Barney (1876-1972)

Novelist and poet who became the most celebrated of the American lesbians exiled in Paris at the end of the 19th century. Barney founded a famous literary salon that lasted for over 60 years.

Romaine Brooks (1874-1970)

American painter exiled in Paris, who became the principal lover of Natalie Barney. Many of her portraits are of members of Barney's salon.

Gertrude Stein (1874-1946)

Writer and art collector of great significance. Stein left America in 1904 and spent the majority of her life in Paris. With her lover Alice B. Toklas, Stein was part of the most famous lesbian duo in the world, in the early 20th century.

Sylvia Beach (1887-1962)

Pioneering bookshop owner and publisher. Beach left America to spend the rest of her life in Paris with her lover Adrienne Monnier. Beach founded the bookshop Shakespeare and Company and was the first publisher of James Joyce's *Ulysses*.

W. H. Auden (1907-73)

English poet who abandoned England for the gay pleasures of Berlin in the 1930s. Auden then moved to America and spent most of the rest of his life there. Respect for Auden's work was tempered by condemnation for his abandonment of his country at a time of war.

Christopher Isherwood (1904-86)

English novelist. Like Auden, Isherwood was attracted to the gay life of Berlin, then moved to California in the early 1940s. He spent the remainder of his life in exile there, writing and studying Hindu mysticism.

Paul Bowles (1910-99)

Novelist and composer who, after exile in Paris, became the doyen of the gay community of Tangier after the Second World War. He was married to lesbian writer Jane Auer.

James Baldwin (1924-87)

Influential American novelist who settled in France, first in Paris and then Provence, to avoid racial prejudice and homophobia. Baldwin was deeply committed to the American Civil Rights Movement, although he never returned to live permanently in America.

BIBLIOGRAPHY

Alexander, Boyd, *Life at Fonthill 1807–1822*, Hart-Davis, London, 1957.

Aquinas, St. Thomas, *Summa Theologia*, Blackfriars, Cambridge, 1964.

Auden, W. H. and Isherwood, Christopher, *Journey to a War*, Faber and Faber, 2002.

Augustine, *City of God against the Pagans*, Tr. R. W. Dyson, Cambridge University Press, Cambridge, 1998.

Augustine, *Confessions*, Tr. H. Chadwick, Oxford University Press, Oxford, 1991.

Axworthy, Michael, *Iran: Empire of the Mind: A History from Zoroaster to the Present Day*, Penguin, London, 2008.

Baer, Brian, *Other Russias: Homosexuality and the Crisis of Post-Soviet Identity*, Palgrave Macmillan, London, 2009.

Bagemihl, Bruce, *Biological Exuberance: Animal Sexuality and Natural Diversity*, St Martin's Press, New York, 1999.

Baldwin, James, *If Beale Street Could Talk*, Penguin, London, 1994.

Bailey, Derrick, *Homosexuality and the Western Christian Tradition*, Longmans, Green, London, 1955.

Barlow, Frank, *William Rufus*, University of California Press, Berkeley, 1983.

Baudri de, Bourgueil, *Les Oeuvres Poétiques*, H. Champion, Paris, 1926

Beckford, William, *The Journals of William Beckford in Portugal and Spain 1787–1788*, Ed. B. Alexander, J. Day, New York, 1955.

BIBLIOGRAPHY

Benkovitz, Miriam, *Frederick Rolfe, Baron Corvo: A Biography*, Putnam, New York, 1977.

Brantome, Pierre de Bourdeille, *The Lives of the Gallant Ladies*, Tr. A. Brown, Elek, London, 1961.

Bray, Alan, *Homosexuality in Renaissance England*, Gay Men's Press, London, 1962.

Brooks, Peter, *Henry James Goes to Paris*, University Press, Princeton, 2007.

Buckley, Veronica, *Christina Queen of Sweden*, Fourth Estate, London, 2004.

Calloway, Stephan, *The Exquisite Life of Oscar Wilde*, Orion Media, London, 1998.

Carpenter, Humphrey, *W. H. Auden: A Biography*, Allen & Unwin, London, 1981.

Castle, Terry, *The Apparitional Lesbian: Female Homosexuality and Modern Culture*, New York University Press, New York, 1993.

Coughlin, Con, *Khomeini's Ghost: Iran Since 1979*, Macmillan, London, 2008.

Crompton, Louis, *Byron and Greek Love: Homophobia in Nineteenth Century England*, University of California Press, Berkeley, 1985.

Crompton, Louis, *Homosexuality and Civilization*, Harvard University Press, Massachusetts, 2006.

Cust, Robert H., *Giovanni Antonio Bazzi, Hitherto Usually Styled 'Sodoma': The Man and the Painter 1477–1549*, John Murray, London, 1906.

Daniel, Walter, *The Life of Ailred of Rievaulx*, Tr. F. M. Powicke, Nelson, London, 1930.

DeJean, Joan, *Fictions of Sappho 1546–1937*, University of Chicago Press, Chicago, 1989.

Dekker, Rudolf M. and van de Pol, Lotte C., *The Traditions of*

Female Transvestism in Early Modern Europe, St. Martin's Press, New York, 1989.

Disney, John, *A Second Essay upon the Execution of the Laws against Immorality and Prophaneness*, J. Dowling, London, 1710.

Donaghue, Emma, *Passions between Women: British Lesbian Culture 1668–1801*, Scarlet Press, London, 1993.

Dover, K. J., *Greek Homosexuality*, Duckworth, London, 1978.

Durham, Martin, *Women and Fascism*, Routledge, London, 1998.

Eadmar, Tr. R. W. Southern, *The Life of St. Anselm, Archbishop of Canterbury*, T. Nelson, London, 1962.

Eckman, Fern Marja, *The Furious Passage of James Baldwin*, Michael Joseph, London, 1968.

Edel, Leon, *The Complete Notebooks of Henry James*, Oxford University Press, Oxford, 1987.

Eglington, J. Z., *Greek Love*, Oliver Layton Press, New York, 1964.

Ellmann, Richard, *Oscar Wilde*, Vintage, London, 1988.

Evans, Richard J., *Rituals of Retribution: Capital Punishment in Germany 1600–1987*, Oxford University Press, Oxford, 1996.

Faderman, Lillian, *Surpassing the Love of Men: Romantic Friendships and Love between Women from the Renaissance to the Present*, William Morrow, New York, 1981.

Field, Andrew, *Djuna: The Life and Times of Djuna Barnes*, Putnam, London, 1983.

Flannery, Edward H., *The Anguish of the Jews: Twenty-Three Centuries of Anti-Semitism*, Paulist Press, New York, 1983.

Fone, Byrne, *Homophobia: A History*, Henry Holt, New York, 2000.

Foster, Jeanette H., *Sex Variant Women in Literature: A Historical and Quantitative Survey*, F. Muller, London, 1958.

BIBLIOGRAPHY

Fothergill, Brian, *Beckford of Fonthill*, Faber, London, 1979.

Garde, Noel, *Jonathan to Gide: The Homosexual in History*, Vantage Press, New York, 1964.

Gibbon, Edward, *The History of the Decline and Fall of the Roman Empire*, 3 vols, Penguin, London, 1994.

Goldsmith, Margaret, *Christina of Sweden: A Psychological Biography*, Doubleday, New York, 1935.

Goldthwaite, Richard A., *The Building of Renaissance Florence: A Social and Economic History*, John Hopkins University Press, Baltimore, 1980.

Graham, Kenneth, *Henry James: A Literary Life*, Macmillan, London, 1995.

Gray, Thomas, *The Correspondence of Thomas Gray*, Ed. P. Toynbee and L. Whibley, 3 vols, Clarendon Press, Oxford, 1935.

Green, Michelle, *The Dream at the End of the World: Paul Bowles and the Literary Renegades in Tangier*, HarperCollins, London, 1991.

Greenberg, David, *The Social Construction of Homosexuality*, University of Chicago Press, Chicago, 1988.

Gregg, Edward, *Queen Anne*, Routledge & Kegan Paul, 1980.

Grosskurth, Phyllis, *Byron: The Flawed Angel*, Hodder & Stoughton, London, 1997.

Hamilton, Bernard, *The Medieval Inquisition*, Holmes & Meier, New York, 1981.

Hammond, N. G. L., *A History of Greece to 322 B.C.*, Clarendon Press, Oxford, 1967.

Harris, John, *The Destruction of Sodom*, Lathum, London, 1628.

Harvey, Paul, Sir, *The Oxford Companion to Classical Literature*, Oxford University Press, Oxford, 1984.

Haslip, Joan, *Marie Antoinette*, Weidenfeld & Nicolson, London, 1988.

Healey, D., *Homosexual Desire in Revolutionary Russia: The Regulation of Sexual and Gender Dissent*, University of Chicago Press, Chicago, 2004.

Herring, Philip, *Djuna: Life and Work of Djuna Barnes*, Viking, London, 1996.

Hibbard, Howard, *Caravaggio*, Harper and Row, New York, 1983.

Holland, Merlin, *Irish Peacock and Scarlet Marquess; The Real Trial of Oscar Wilde*, Fourth Estate, London, 2003.

Hyde, H. Montgomery, *Henry James at Home*, Methuen, London, 1969.

Hynes, Samuel, *The Auden Generation; Literature and Politics in England in the 1930s*, Pimlico, London, 1992.

Isherwood, Christopher, *The Memorial: Portrait of a Family*, Hogarth Press, London, 1952.

Isherwood, Christopher, *Christopher and His Kind*, University of Minnesota Press, Minnesota, 2001.

James, Henry, *Henry James: A Life in Letters*, Ed. Philip Horne, Allen Lane, London, 1999.

Janson, H. W., *The Sculptures of Donatello*, Princeton University Press, Princeton, 1963.

Kelen, Emery, *Mr. Nonsense: A Life of Edward Lear*, Macdonald and Jane's, London, 1974.

Kelly, J. N. D., *The Oxford Dictionary of Popes*, Oxford University Press, Oxford, 1986.

Ketton-Cremer, Robert Windham, *Thomas Gray: A Biography*, Cambridge University Press, Cambridge, 1955.

Knox, Melissa, *Oscar Wilde, A Long and Lovely Suicide*, Yale University Press, New Haven, 1996.

Lambert, Royston, *Beloved and God: The Story of Hadrian and Antinous*, Viking, London, 1984.

Lea, Henry Charles, *A History of the Inquisition in Spain*, 4 vols, Macmillan, London, 1906–1907.

Lear, Edward, *Selected Letters*, Ed. Vivien Noakes, Oxford University Press, Oxford, 1988.

Legman, G., *The Guilt of the Templars*, Basic Books, New York, 1966.

Levi, Peter, *Edward Lear: A Biography*, Macmillan, London, 1995.

L'Estiole, Pierre, *Journal pour la Régne de Henri III*, Ed. L-R. Lefévre, Gallimard, Paris, 1943.

Licht, Hans, *Sexual Life in Ancient Greece*, Tr. J. H. Freese, The Abbey Library, London, 1932.

Liebert, Robert, *Michelangelo: A Psychoanalytic Study of his Life and Images*, Yale University Press, New Haven, 1983.

Lightbown, Ronald, *Botticelli: Life and Work*, Abbeville Press, New York, 1989.

Lockyer, Roger, *Buckingham: The Life and Political Career of George Villiers, First Duke of Buckingham*, Longman, London, 1981.

Maber, R. G., *Malherbe, Théophile de Viau, and Saint-Amant, A Selection*, University of Durham Press, Durham, 1983.

McBride, Dwight, *James Baldwin Now*, New York University Press, New York, 1999.

MacCarthy, Fiona, *Byron: Life and Legend*, John Murray, London, 2002.

McGann, Jerome, *Byron and Romanticism*, Cambridge University Press, Cambridge, 2002.

McKenna, Neil, *The Secret Life of Oscar Wilde*, Random House, New York, 2004.

McLynn, Frank, *Crime and Punishment in Eighteenth-Century*

England, Thames and Hudson, 1977.

Mayd, Hooman, *The Ayatollah Begs to Differ*, Doubleday Books, New York, 2008.

Malcolm, Janet, *Two Lives: Gertrude and Alice*, Yale University Press, New Haven, 2007.

Masson, Georgina, *Queen Christina*, Farrar, Strauss & Giroux, New York, 1968.

Mavor, Elizabeth, *The Ladies of Llangollen*, Michael Joseph, London, 1971.

Michelangelo, *The Letters of Michelangelo*, Tr. E. H. Ramsden, 2 vols, New York University Press, New York, 1965.

Miller, John, *The Life and Times of William and Mary*, Weidenfeld & Nicolson, London, 1974.

Monter, William, *Frontiers of Heresy: The Spanish Inquisition from the Basque Lands to Sicily*, Cambridge University Press, Cambridge, 1990.

Moote, Lloyd A., *Louis XIII, the Just*, University of California Press, Berkeley, 1989.

Murray, Stephen, *Homosexualities*, University of Chicago Press, Chicago, 2000.

Neumann, Alfred, *The Life of Queen Christina of Sweden*, Hutchinson, London, 1936.

Newcastle, Margaret Cavendish, Duchess of, *Plays, Never Before Printed*, Maxwell, London, 1668.

Noakes, Vivien, *Edward Lear: The Life of a Wanderer*, Collins, London, 1968.

Norton, Rictor, *Mother Clap's Molly House: Gay Subculture in England 1700–1830*, GMP Publishers, London, 1992.

Oosterhuis, Harry, *Homosexuality and Male Bonding in Pre-Nazi Germany: The Youth Movement, the Gay Movement and Male*

Bonding Before Hitler's Rise, Haworth Press, Haworth, 2008.

Oueijan, Naji B., *A Compendium of Eastern Elements in Byron's Oriental Tales*, Peter Lang Publishing, New York, 1999.

Payer, Pierre, *Sex and the Penitentials: The Development of a Sexual Code 550–1150*, University of Toronto Press, Toronto, 1984.

Pearce, Joseph, *The Unmasking of Oscar Wilde*, HarperCollins, London, 2000.

Pedretti, Carlo, *Leonardo: A Study in Chronology and Style*, University of California Press, Berkeley, 1973.

Percy, William, *Pederasty and Pedagogy in Archaic Greece*, University of Illinois Press, Urbana.

Plant, Richard, *The Pink Triangle; The Nazi War against Homosexuals*, Henry Holt, New York, 1986.

Plato, *The Dialogues of Plato*, Tr. B. Jowett, Oxford University Press, Oxford, 1953.

Pope-Henessy, John, *Cellini*, Abbeville Press, New York, 1985.

The Pursuit of Sodomy: Male Homosexuality in Renaissance and Enlightenment Europe, Ed. K. Gerard and G. Hemka, Haworth Press, New York, 1989.

Raby, Peter (ed.), *The Cambridge Companion to Oscar Wilde*, Cambridge University Press, Cambridge, 1997.

Rochester, John Wilmot, Earl of, *Collected Works*, Ed J. Hayward, Nonesuch, London, 1926.

Rochester, John Wilmot, Earl of, *Sodomy, or the Quintessence of Debauchery*, Olympia Press, Paris, 1957.

Rocke, Michael, *Forbidden Friendships: Homosexuality and Male Culture in Renaissance Florence*, Oxford University Press, Oxford, 1996.

Roditi, Edouard, *Oscar Wilde*, New Directions, London, 1986.

BIBLIOGRAPHY

Rodriguez, Suzanne, *Wild Heart: A Life: Natalie Barney and the Decadence of Literary Paris*, Harper Perennial, London, 2003.

Rosen, Fred, *Bentham, Byron and Greece*, Clarendon Press, Oxford, 1992.

Rowbothom, Sheila, *Edward Carpenter: A Life of Liberty and Love*, Verso, London, 2008.

Ruggiero, Guido, *The Boundaries of Eros: Sex Crime and Sexuality in Renaissance Venice*, Oxford University Press, Oxford, 1985.

Sappho, *Sappho of Lesbos: Her Works Restored*, Tr. B. Saklatvala, Skilton, London, 1968.

Schenkar, Joan, *Truly Wilde: The Unsettling Story of Oscar's Unusual Niece*, Virago, London, 2000.

Senelick, Lawrence, *The Changing Room; Sex, Drag and Theatre*, Routledge, New York, 2000.

Seymour, Miranda, *A Ring of Conspirators: Henry James and his Literary Circle 1895–1915*, Hodder & Stoughton, 1988.

Shaw, Christine, *Julius II: The Warrior Pope*, Blackwell, Oxford, 1993.

Smith, Bruce R., *Homosexual Desire in Shakespeare's England: A Cultural Poetics*, University of Chicago Press, Chicago, 1991.

The Sodomites Shame and Doom, J. Dawning, London, 1702.

Souhami, Diana, *Gertrude and Alice*, Pandora, London, 1991.

Souhami, Diana, *Wild Girls: Natalie Barney and Romaine Brooks*, Phoenix, London, 2005.

Southern, R. W., *Saint Anselm: A Portrait in a Landscape*, Cambridge University Press, Cambridge, 1990.

Steakley, James, *The Homosexual Emancipation Movement in Germany*, Arno, New York, 1975.

Stearns, Peter, *Sexuality in World History*, Routledge, London, 2009.

Stein, Gertrude, *Paris, France: Personal Recollections*, Peter Owen, London, 1971.

Stehling, Thomas, *Medieval Latin Poems of Love and Friendship*, Garland, New York, 1984.

Stewart, Andrew, *Art, Desire and the Body in Ancient Greece*, Cambridge University Press, Cambridge, 1997.

Suetonius, Tr. J. C. Rolfe, 2 vols, Harvard University Press, Massachusetts, 1913.

Symons, A. J. A, *The Quest for Corvo: An Experiment in Biography*, New York Review, 2001.

Symonds, John Addington, *The Life of Michelangelo Buonarroti*, 2 vols, C.Scribner's Sons, New York, 1911.

Symonds, John Addington, 'A problem in Greek Ethics.' In *Sexual Inversion*, Ed. H. Ellis and J. A. Symonds, Arno, New York, 1975

Symonds, John Addington, *The Renaissance in Italy*, Henry Holt, New York, 1912.

Symonds, John Addington, *Portraits and Anecdotes*, Tr. H. Miles, Oxford University Press, Oxford, 1965.

Takeyh, Ray, *Hidden Iran: Paradox and Power in the Islamic Republic*, Henry Holt, New York, 2007.

The Third Pink Book: A Global View of Lesbian and Gay Liberation and Oppression, Ed. A. Hendricks, R. Tielman and E. Van der Veen, Prometheus Books, Buffalo, 1993.

Trevisan, Jao, *Perverts in Paradise*, Tr. M. Foreman, GMP Publishers, London, 1986.

Van Kleffens, E. N., *Hispanic Law until the End of the Middle Ages*, Edinburgh University Press, Edinburgh, 1968.

Vasari, Giorgio, *The Lives of the Painters, Sculptors and Architects*, Tr. A. B. Hinds, 4 vols, Dutton, New York, 1963.

Viau, Théophile de, *The Cabaret Poetry of Théophile de Viau*, Ed. C.

L. Gaudiano, J-M. Place, Paris, 1981.

Walpole, Horace, *The Yale Edition of Horace Wapole's Correspondence*, ed. W. S. Lewis, 42 vols, Yale University Press, New Haven, 1937-1980.

Weeks, Donald, *Corvo*, Michael Joseph, London, 1971.

Weeks, Jeffrey, *Coming Out: Homosexual Politics in Britain from the Nineteenth Century to the Present*, Quartet Books, London, 1977.

Wilde, Oscar, *Complete Letters of Oscar Wilde*, Ed. M. Holland, Fourth Estate, London, 2000.

Wilde, Oscar, *The Complete Works of Oscar Wilde*, Collins, London, 2003.

The Trials of Oscar Wilde 1895, Stationery Office Books, London, 2002.

Williams, Craig, *Roman Homosexuality: Ideologies of Masculinity in Classical Antiquity*, Oxford University Press, Oxford, 1999.

Williams, H. Noel, *Later Queens of the French Stage*, C. Scribner's Sons, New York, 1906.

Wineapple, Brenda, *Sister Brother: Gertrude and Leo Stein*, Bloomsbury, London, 1996.

Wood, Julia, *The Resurrection of Oscar Wilde*, The Lutterworth Press, London, 2007.

Yates, Jim, *Oh! Pére Lachaise: Oscar's Wilde Purgatory*, Édition d'Amélie, Paris, 2007.

Young, Michael, *James I and the History of Homosexuality*, Macmillan, London, 2000.

Yves de Chartres, *Correspondence*, Tr. J. Leclerq, 2 vols, Belles Lettres, Paris, 1949.

Zaborowska, Magdalena, *James Baldwin's Turkish Decade: Erotics of Exile*, Duke University Press, North Carolina, 2008.

LIST OF ILLUSTRATIONS

Front cover image: Paul Bowles (1910–99), circa 1947 in Tangier. © Condé Nast Archive/Corbis.

Plate 1. Benvenuto Cellini (1500–71) © Time & Life Pictures/ Getty Images.

Plate 2. Thomas Gray (1716–71), circa 1770. © Getty Images.

Plate 3. King Henry III of France (1551–89), by Francois Quesnel. © Getty Images.

Plate 4. The Ladies of Llangollen: Eleanor Butler (1739–1829) and Sarah Ponsonby (1755–1831). © Alex Ramsay Photography.

Plate 5. William Beckford (1760–1844), mezzotint after Sir Joshua Reynolds. © The Granger Collection/Topfoto.

Plate 6. Lord Byron (1788–1824), circa 1810. © Getty Images.

Plate 7. Edward Lear (1812–88) and Chichester Fortescue (1823–98), in September 1857. © Hulton-Deutsch Collection/ Corbis.

Plate 8. John Addington (A. J.) Symonds (1840–93), circa 1880s. © Bettmann/Corbis.

Plate 9. Oscar Wilde (1854–1900), photographed during his stay in America in the 1880s. © Bettmann/Corbis.

Plate 10. W. H. Auden (1907–73) and Christopher Isherwood (1904–86) in January 1938, leaving London, England, on their journey to China. © Bettmann/Corbis.

Plate 11. Henry James (1843–1916). © Bettmann/Corbis.

Plate 12. Gertrude Stein (1874–1946) in Paris, France, in March 1930, seated before a portrait of herself that was painted by Spanish artist Pablo Picasso (1881–1973). © Bettmann/Corbis.

Plate 13. James Baldwin (1924–87), photographed on 20 January 1986 in Paris, France. © Julio Donoso/Corbis Sygma.

INDEX

INDEX

INDEX